Key Stage 2 Maths

CW01582148

WORKBOOK 1

Numerical Reasoning Technique

Dr Stephen C Curran
with Autumn McMahon
Edited by Katrina MacKay

This book belongs to

ae PUBLICATIONS
Accelerated Education Publications Ltd

Contents

Chapter One
BASIC NUMBER
1. Tens Number System

The **Tens Number System** is also called the **Denary System**.

- Single figures are termed **digits**.
- Groups of digits are termed **numbers**.
- **Place value** means that the position of a digit in any number represents its value.

	T/Th/Th	Th/Th	H/Th	T/Th	Th	H	T	U
Ten million (ten thousand thousands) ←	1	0	0	0	0	0	0	0
One million (thousand thousands) ←		1	0	0	0	0	0	0
One hundred thousand ←			1	0	0	0	0	0
Ten thousand ←				1	0	0	0	0
One thousand ←					1	0	0	0
One hundred ←						1	0	0
Ten ←							1	0
One ←								1

Key

U - Units
T - Tens
H - Hundreds
Th - Thousands

←

One hundred ←	1	0	0
Ten ←		1	0
One ←			1

Going from right to left each column is ten times greater than the previous.

10 × 10 = 100

10 × 1 = 10

Start with **1**

a. Numbers in Figures

Example: Write four hundred and fifty-five thousand and seven in figures.

Place the number in the table (start in **100,000** column).

Answer: **455,007**

Exercise 1: 1 Write the numbers in figures:

1) Sixty-eight = ______
2) Eight hundred and eighteen = ______
3) Five hundred thousand = ______
4) Five hundred and sixty-eight = ______
5) One thousand and eighty-one = ______
6) Forty-six thousand = ______
7) Seven thousand, eight hundred and eighty-four = ______
8) Two hundred and four thousand, eight hundred and forty = ______
9) Eleven thousand = ______
10) Five million, eight hundred and twenty thousand, five hundred and twenty-nine = ______

Score Out of Ten →

b. Numbers in Writing

Example: Write **9,590** in words.

Place the number in the table (start in **1,000** column).

Answer: **Nine thousand, five hundred and ninety**

Exercise 1: 2 Put the figures into writing:

Score

1) **31** = ____________________

2) **69** = ____________________

3) **296** = ____________________

4) **590** = ____________________

5) **529** = ____________________

6) **4,786** = ____________________

7) **35,701** = ____________________

8) **57,450** = ____________________

9) **964,402** = ____________________

10) **2,093,482** = ____________________

c. Number Values

Exercise 1: 3 Calculate the following:

1) Rearrange these numbers in size order, largest first.

1,364 463 7,450 9,886 194 3,211

______ ______ ______ ______ ______ ______

Write the value of the underlined figures.

2) In writing:

59,4$\underline{1}$6 $\underline{9}$30

______ ______

3) In numbers:

$\underline{8}$8,361 1$\underline{7}$ 27$\underline{8}$, 296

______ ______ ______

4) Which is largest?

265,922 or **212,276**

______

5) Which is smallest?

87,506 or **83,323**

______

6) Write out all the numbers that can be made from **569** in size order, largest first (the first is done).

965 ______ ______ ______ ______ ______

7) Which is smallest?

379,899 or **327,619**

______

8) Which is largest?

23,115 or **29,033**

______

9) Rearrange these numbers in size order, smallest first.

1,526 99 7,870 786 33 8,701

______ ______ ______ ______ ______ ______

10) What is the smallest number that can be made from **69,263**? ______

Score

2. Addition

Example: Calculate 509 + 192.

```
  5 0 9     ← Start here
              9 + 2 = 11
  1 9 2 +
  -------
  7 0 1       Carry ten to
  -------
   1  1   ←   next column.
```

Answer: **701**

Exercise 1: 4a

1)
```
 6 0 3 5
 1 2 9 2 +
 ________

 ________
```

2)
```
 7 5 3 4
 1 6 6 0 +
 ________

 ________
```

3)
```
 6 5 1 9
 4 3 7 2 +
 ________

 ________
```

4)
```
 7 8 1 1
 4 9 9 8 +
 ________

 ________
```

Addition is a commutative operation; **2** + **3** gives the same answer as **3** + **2**.

Addition Terms

- Add
- Plus
- Total
- Both
- Increase
- Enlarge
- Find the total of
- Find the sum of
- More than
- Combine
- Altogether
- In all

If numbers are missing.
Example:

```
  2 □ 2
  3 7 [8] +
  -------
  □ 9 0
  -------
      1
```

2 + **?** = **10**
Missing number must be **8**.

```
  2 [1] 2
  3 7 [8] +
  -------
  [5] 9 0
  -------
      1
```

Follow the normal stages of addition.

Exercise 1: 4b

Score

5)
```
  □ 6 1
  2 7 □ +
  -------
 1 2 □ 9
```

6)
```
  8 □ 2
  1 8 5 +
  -------
 □ 0 4 □
```

7)
```
  7 9 □ 9
  2 0 0 3 +
  --------
  □ □ 2 2
```

8)
```
  8 1 □ 5
  5 □ 6 9 +
  --------
 1 3 6 8 □
```

9)
```
  □ 3 0 5
  6 8 9 □ +
  --------
 1 3 □ 0 3
```

10)
```
  □ 7 3 □
  1 4 8 6 +
  --------
 1 1 2 □ 8
```

3. Subtraction
a. Method One

The standard method involves **borrowing from the top**.

Example: Calculate **548 – 99.**

8 subtract **9** cannot be done.
Borrow **10** from **40**.
Cross out **4** and make it **3**.
8 becomes **18** (**10** + **8**) then subtract.
Continue same method to the end.

```
 4 13 1
 5̸ 4̸ 8
    9 9 –
 ───────
  4 4 9
 ───────
```

Answer: **449**

Exercise 1: 5a Calculate the following:

1)	2)	3)	4)
8192	**9570**	**8856**	**7435**
1784 –	**359** –	**2469** –	**1948** –
______	______	______	______

Subtraction is not commutative; **2** – **3** is not the same as **3** – **2**.

Subtraction Terms

- Subtract
- Deduct
- Remove
- Take away/from/off
- Less
- Decrease
- Discount
- Find the difference
- Minus
- Reduce
- Dock
- Debit

Example: Calculate **300 – 216.**

0 subtract **6** cannot be done.
There are **0 tens** so borrow from the hundreds column instead of the tens column. Take **100** from **300**, leaving **200** (cross out **3**, write **2**).
Use the **100** to fill up tens & units column.
90 in the tens (cross out **0**, write **9**) and
10 in the units (write **1**, making **10**).

```
 2 9 1
 3̸ 0̸ 0
 2 1 6 –
 ───────
 0 8 4
 ───────
```

Answer: **84**

Exercise 1: 5b Calculate the following:

Score

5) $\begin{array}{r} 800 \\ 765 - \\ \hline \\ \hline \end{array}$

6) $\begin{array}{r} 500 \\ 293 - \\ \hline \\ \hline \end{array}$

7) $\begin{array}{r} 9000 \\ 5384 - \\ \hline \\ \hline \end{array}$

8) $\begin{array}{r} 3009 \\ 495 - \\ \hline \\ \hline \end{array}$

9) $\begin{array}{r} 4500 \\ 1029 - \\ \hline \\ \hline \end{array}$

10) $\begin{array}{r} 6003 \\ 2166 - \\ \hline \\ \hline \end{array}$

b. Method Two

A second method involves **adding to the bottom**.

Example: Calculate **1,000 – 546**.

0 subtract **6** cannot be done.
Borrow **10** and pay back.
Make **0** into **10**. Add **1** to **4** making **5**.
Continue method to end of calculation.

$$\begin{array}{r} {}^{0}\not{1}\;{}^{1}0\;{}^{1}0\;{}^{1}0 \\ {}^{6}\not{5}\;{}^{5}\not{4}\;6\;- \\ \hline 454 \\ \hline \end{array}$$

Answer: **454**

Exercise 1: 6 Calculate the following:

1) $\begin{array}{r} 1000 \\ 785 - \\ \hline \\ \hline \end{array}$

2) $\begin{array}{r} 1000 \\ 411 - \\ \hline \\ \hline \end{array}$

3) $\begin{array}{r} 1000 \\ 342 - \\ \hline \\ \hline \end{array}$

4) $\begin{array}{r} 7000 \\ 732 - \\ \hline \\ \hline \end{array}$

5) $\begin{array}{r} 8010 \\ 277 - \\ \hline \\ \hline \end{array}$

6) $\begin{array}{r} 6400 \\ 2868 - \\ \hline \\ \hline \end{array}$

7) $\begin{array}{r} 9050 \\ 4865 - \\ \hline \\ \hline \end{array}$

8) $\begin{array}{r} 6002 \\ 557 - \\ \hline \\ \hline \end{array}$

9) $\begin{array}{r} 65830 \\ 54442 - \\ \hline \\ \hline \end{array}$

10) $\begin{array}{r} 40000 \\ 7462 - \\ \hline \\ \hline \end{array}$

Score

Missing numbers are found using methods one and two.

Example:

4	1	2	□	
□	5	□	3	−
1	□	6	8	

~~4~~ 3	~~1~~ 10	~~2~~ 11	1 (1)	
2	~~5~~ 6	5	3	−
1	5	6	8	

? – 3 = 8 (Missing number is **1**.)
Make the **2** in next column into **1**.
Borrow **1**, making **11**.
11 – ? = 6 (Missing number is **5**.)
Pay back **1**; make the **5** into **6**.
Borrow **1**, making **10**.
Make **4** in the next column into **3**.
10 – 6 = ? (Missing number is **4**.)
3 – ? = 2 (Missing number is **1**.)

Exercise 1: 7

Calculate the following:

1)

5	□	3	
□	5	□	−
2	4	9	

2)

□	8	6	
2	□	9	−
1	9	□	

3)

7	□	2	
5	1	□	−
□	8	5	

4)

□	0	7	
4	□	8	−
1	3	□	

5)

7	8	1	□	
3	□	8	6	−
□	8	□	1	

6)

9	□	9	4	
□	9	5	□	−
5	9	□	7	

7)

9	□	5	□	
7	9	□	9	−
□	5	8	0	

8)

8	□	9	3	
□	9	□	4	−
5	9	7	□	

9)

□	3	□	6	
1	0	5	□	−
1	□	4	8	

10)

□	9	5	□	
1	□	8	7	−
3	7	□	8	

Score

4. Multiplication

a. Short Multiplication

This method is used when **Multiplying** by single digits (**1**-**9**).

Example: Calculate **469** × **4**.

9 × **4** = **36** Carry **3** and write **6**.
6 × **4** = **24** Add **3**. **24** + **3** = **27**
Carry **2** and write **7**. **4** × **4** = **16**
Add **2**. **16** + **2** = **18**

$$\begin{array}{r} 469 \\ 4\times \\ \hline 1876 \\ \hline {}_{2\ 3} \end{array}$$

Answer: **1,876**

Exercise 1: 8a Calculate the following:

Score

1) $\begin{array}{r} 7191 \\ 9\times \\ \hline \\ \hline \end{array}$

2) $\begin{array}{r} 5465 \\ 7\times \\ \hline \\ \hline \end{array}$

3) $\begin{array}{r} 8255 \\ 3\times \\ \hline \\ \hline \end{array}$

4) $\begin{array}{r} 7513 \\ 6\times \\ \hline \\ \hline \end{array}$

5) $\begin{array}{r} 2381 \\ 5\times \\ \hline \\ \hline \end{array}$

6) $\begin{array}{r} 7211 \\ 4\times \\ \hline \\ \hline \end{array}$

Finding missing numbers.

Example:

$$\begin{array}{r} 68\square \\ 2\times \\ \hline \square 368 \\ \hline \end{array}$$

$$\begin{array}{r} 68\boxed{4} \\ 2\times \\ \hline \boxed{1}368 \\ \hline {}_{1} \end{array}$$

2 × **?** = **8**
It must be
2 × **4** = **8**

Do as a normal multiplication.

Exercise 1: 8b

7) $\begin{array}{r} 204 \\ \square\times \\ \hline \square 020 \\ \hline \end{array}$

8) $\begin{array}{r} 82\square \\ 9\times \\ \hline 7\square 34 \\ \hline \end{array}$

9) $\begin{array}{r} 9\square 7 \\ 7\times \\ \hline 669\square \\ \hline \end{array}$

10) $\begin{array}{r} \square 36 \\ 8\times \\ \hline 668\square \\ \hline \end{array}$

Multiplication Terms

- Find the product of
- Repeated Addition
- Multiply
- Times
- Scale up by
- Number of sets/groups/lots of
- Double (multiply by **2**)
- Treble/Triple (multiply by **3**)
- Quadruple (multiply by **4**)

- The number being multiplied is the **multiplicand**.
- The multiplying number is the **multiplier**.
- The number obtained is the **product**.

$$\begin{array}{r} 89 \leftarrow \text{Multiplicand} \\ \text{Multiplier} \searrow \; 9\times \\ \hline 801 \leftarrow \text{Product} \\ \hline \end{array}$$

Multiplication is a commutative operation; **3** × **2** gives the same answer as **2** × **3**.

b. Multiplying by Tens

To multiply by **10**, put **0** on the end. **5** × **10** = **50**

To multiply by **100**, put **00** on the end. **5** × **100** = **500**

To multiply by **1,000**, put **000** on the end. **5** × **1,000** = **5,000**

Example: Calculate **100** × **5,000**.

Count the number of zeros on the multiplier and put the same number of zeros on the muliplicand.

Answer: **100** × **5,000** = **500,000**

Exercise 1: 9 Calculate the following: **Score**

1) **4** × **10** = ________
2) **9** × **100** = ________
3) **8** × **1,000** = ________
4) **27** × **100** = ________
5) **10** × **70** = ________
6) **100** × **800** = ________
7) **100** × **130** = ________
8) **1,000** × **33** = ________
9) **100** × **92** = ________
10) **10** × **3,000** = ________

c. Long Multiplication

Long Multiplication is used when multiplying by more than one digit.

Method 1 - This involves breaking the sum into two distinct parts.

Example: Calculate **842** × **93**.

Step 1 - Multiply **842** by the **3** units as in short multiplication.

$$\begin{array}{r} 842 \\ 3\times \\ \hline 2526 \\ \hline \end{array}$$

(carry: 1)

Step 2 - Multiply the **90** units (nine tens). Place a **0** in the first space as the units have been multiplied already.

$$\begin{array}{r} 842 \\ \nwarrow \uparrow \nearrow \\ 90\times \\ \hline 75780 \\ \hline \end{array}$$

(carries: 3, 1)

Step 3 - Add the two results together to attain the answer.

$$\begin{array}{r} 2526 \\ 75780+ \\ \hline 78306 \\ \hline \end{array}$$

(carries: 1, 1)

Answer: **78,306**

Exercise 1: 10 Calculate the following:

Score

1) Multiply **68** by **31**.

$$\begin{array}{r} 68 \\ 1\times \\ \hline \\ \hline \end{array} \quad + \quad \begin{array}{r} 68 \\ 30\times \\ \hline 0 \\ \hline \end{array}$$

Add the two sums to find the answer. ____________

2) Multiply **75** by **44**.

$$\begin{array}{r} 75 \\ 4\times \\ \hline \\ \hline \end{array} \quad + \quad \begin{array}{r} 75 \\ 40\times \\ \hline 0 \\ \hline \end{array}$$

Add the two sums to find the answer. ____________

3) Multiply **87** by **21**.

```
 8 7        8 7
   1 ×      2 0 ×
_____      _____
         +    0
_____      _____
```

Answer ____________

4) Multiply **81** by **49**.

```
 8 1        8 1
   9 ×      4 0 ×
_____      _____
         +    0
_____      _____
```

Answer ____________

5) Multiply **451** by **95**.

```
 4 5 1      4 5 1
     5 ×      9 0 ×
______     ______
         +      0
______     ______
```

Answer ____________

6) Multiply **962** by **46**.

```
 9 6 2      9 6 2
     6 ×      4 0 ×
______     ______
         +      0
______     ______
```

Answer ____________

7) Multiply **458** by **85**.

```
 4 5 8      4 5 8
     5 ×      8 0 ×
______     ______
         +      0
______     ______
```

Answer ____________

8) Multiply **471** by **56**.

```
 4 7 1      4 7 1
     6 ×      5 0 ×
______     ______
         +      0
______     ______
```

Answer ____________

9) Multiply **2705** by **36**.

```
 2 7 0 5      2 7 0 5
       6 ×        3 0 ×
________     ________
           +        0
________     ________
```

Answer ____________

10) Multiply **7690** by **89**.

```
 7 6 9 0      7 6 9 0
       9 ×        8 0 ×
________     ________
           +        0
________     ________
```

Answer ____________

Method 2 - The traditional method combines both sums and can be used when multiplying by more than one digit.

Example: Calculate **842** × **93**.

Ignore the **9** and multiply by **3**.

Line 1 - **3** × **842** = **2,526**

Now multiply by **9** (see arrows).

Line 2 - Put a **0** in units column.

- **90** × **842** = **75,780**

Add Line 1 and Line 2 = Line 3.

2,526 + **75,780** = **78,306**

Answer: **78,306**

$$
\begin{array}{rl}
8\,4\,2 & \\
\nwarrow \uparrow \nearrow & \\
9\,3\,\times & \\
\hline
2\,5\,2\,6 & \text{Line 1} \\
+\,7\,5\,7\,8\,0 & \text{Line 2} \\
\hline
7\,8\,3\,0\,6 & \text{Line 3} \\
\hline
\end{array}
$$

Exercise 1: 11 Calculate the following:

Score

1) 72 × 23 = ______ (Line 2: ____0)

2) 45 × 16 = ______ (Line 2: ____0)

3) 79 × 24 = ______ (Line 2: ____0)

4) 64 × 26 = ______ (Line 2: ____0)

5) 156 × 72 = ______

6) 732 × 96 = ______

7) 798 × 34 = ______

8) 3318 × 29 = ______

9) 5637 × 36 = ______

10) 6184 × 71 = ______

5. Division
a. Short Division

This method is used when **Dividing** by a single digit.

Example: Calculate **493 ÷ 8**.

8 divides into **49** six times, remainder **1**.
Write **6** and carry the **1**.
8 divides into **13** once, remainder **5**.
Write **1** and put a remainder of **5**.

$$\begin{array}{r} 6\;1 \text{ r. 5} \\ 8\,\overline{)\,4\;9\;{}^{1}3} \end{array}$$

Answer: **61 r. 5**

Exercise 1: 12a Calculate the following:

(Questions 1-3 have no remainders.)

1) $9\,\overline{)\,6\;2\;1}$ 2) $6\,\overline{)\,9\;3\;6}$ 3) $4\,\overline{)\,2\;8\;4}$

(Questions 4-6 have remainders.)

4) $7\,\overline{)\,7\;3\;8\;2}$ 5) $6\,\overline{)\,2\;3\;1\;7}$ 6) $8\,\overline{)\,4\;2\;7\;2\;5}$

If numbers are missing do the following:

Example:

$$\begin{array}{r} \square\;1 \text{ r. 5} \\ 9\,\overline{)\,5\;5\;4} \end{array} \qquad \begin{array}{r} \boxed{6}\;1 \text{ r. 5} \\ 9\,\overline{)\,5\;5\;4} \end{array}$$

Answer: The missing number must be **6**.

Exercise 1: 12b Fill in the missing numbers:

Score

7) $\begin{array}{r} 1\;0\;\square\;4 \\ 6\,\overline{)\,6\;0\;8\;4} \end{array}$ 8) $\begin{array}{r} 2\;\square\;4\;0 \\ 3\,\overline{)\,6\;4\;2\;0} \end{array}$

9) $\begin{array}{r} 5\;1\;6 \\ 8\,\overline{)\,4\;1\;2\;\square} \end{array}$ 10) $\begin{array}{r} 6\;3\;3 \\ 6\,\overline{)\,3\;\square\;9\;8} \end{array}$

Division Terms

- Share
- Divide
- Find the quotient
- Partition

To find:

- a half, divide by **2**.
- a third, divide by **3**.
- a quarter/fourth, divide by **4**.
- a fifth, divide by **5**.

- The number being divided into is the **dividend**.
- The dividing number is the **divisor** or **divider**.
- The number obtained is the **quotient**.
- The left over is the **remainder**.

Quotient → **2 6 r. 1** ← Remainder

Divisor → **3 | 7 ¹9** ← Dividend

b. Dividing by Tens

To divide by **10**, remove **0**. **30 ÷ 10 = 3**

To divide by **100**, remove **00**. **300 ÷ 100 = 3**

To divide by **1,000**, remove **000**. **3,000 ÷ 1,000 = 3**

Example: Calculate **5,000 ÷ 100**.

Count the number of zeros on the divisor and remove the same number of zeros from the dividend.

Answer: **5,000 ÷ 100 = 50**

Exercise 1: 13 Calculate the following: **Score**

1) **20 ÷ 10** = _______
2) **700 ÷ 100** = _______
3) **9,000 ÷ 100** = _______
4) **440 ÷ 10** = _______
5) **500 ÷ 100** = _______
6) **3,900 ÷ 10** = _______
7) **800 ÷ 10** = _______
8) **650 ÷ 10** = _______
9) **7,000 ÷ 100** = _______
10) **4,200 ÷ 100** = _______

c. Long Division

This method is used when dividing by two digits.

Example: Calculate **3,829** ÷ **16**.

3 cannot be divided by **16**.

16 divides into **38** twice.

Write **2** in the answer.

2 × **16** = **32**

Write **32** under **38**.

Subtract **38** – **32** = **6**.

Bring down the **2**.

To help divide use:
<u>D</u>addy
<u>M</u>ummy
<u>S</u>ister
<u>B</u>rother
(D - divide)
(M - multiply)
(S - subtract)
(B - bring down)

```
        2 3 9  r. 5
16 | 3 8 2 9
     3 2 ↓ ↓
       6 2
       4 8
       1 4 9
       1 4 4
           5
```

Subtract to find the remainders.

16 divides into **62** three times.

Put a **3** in the answer.

3 × **16** = **48**

Subtract **62** – **48** = **14**

Bring down the **9**.

16 divides into **149** by **9** (rough work).

Write **9** in the answer. **9** × **16** = **144**

Write **144** under **149** and subtract.

16 will not divide into **5**.

There is a remainder of **5**.

Answer: **239 r. 5**

Rough Work

Guess and test

16 × 8 = 128	16 × 9 = 144

Only up to 9× per number

In **Long Division**, remainders are found by subtracting on paper instead of using mental calculations (the only difference between long and short division).

Exercise 1: 14

Calculate the following:
(Questions 1- 4 have no remainders.)

1) **15 | 3 4 6 5**

= ________

2) **19 | 9 9 5 6**

= ________

3) $19\overline{)1596}$ = ________

4) $17\overline{)4012}$ = ________

5) $18\overline{)7194}$ = ________

6) $23\overline{)1448}$ = ________

7) $17\overline{)11969}$ = ________

8) $23\overline{)27271}$ = ________

9) $24\overline{)41454}$ = ________

10) $21\overline{)51927}$ = ________

Score

6. Words to Number Problems

Questions can involve changing words into one or more of the **Four Rules of Number**. + − × ÷

Reminder of the terms: **Addition**; **Subtraction**; **Multiplication**; **Division**

Example: Add the product of **7** and **11** to the sum of **7** and **11** and the difference between **7** and **11**.

Look for the starting point. It is necessary to do each separate sum before adding up all the answers.

Step 1 - The product of **7** and **11**.	$\mathbf{7 \times 11 = 77}$
Step 2 - The sum of **7** and **11**.	$\mathbf{7 + 11 = 18}$
Step 3 - The difference between **7** and **11**.	$\mathbf{11 - 7 = \ 4}$ +
Step 4 - Add the answers to the three parts.	**99**

Answer: **99**

Exercise 1: 15 Answer the following:

Score

1) Find the difference between the quotient of **18** and **3** and the product of **18** and **3**. _______

2) Find the sum of the first ten prime numbers. _______

3) How many times can **34** be subtracted from **2,189**? _______

4) Deduct **26** from **68**, then add **53**. _______

5) Double **18** and then reduce it by **15**. _______

6) Treble **47** and take away **16**. _______

7) Halve **36** and add **6**. Then multiply this by **4**. _______

8) Decrease **12** by **4** and divide by **4**. _______

9) Quadruple **5** and subtract **2**. Divide this by **3**. _______

10) What is the sum of the numbers here that are divisible by **6**? _______ **187**, **456**, **346**, **263**, **966**

7. Inverse Operations

It is useful to understand the relationship between the Four Rules of Number. **Inverse means opposite.**

+ and – are a pair of inverse operations.

$3 + 8 = \mathbf{11}$; $11 - 3 = \mathbf{8}$; $11 - 8 = \mathbf{3}$

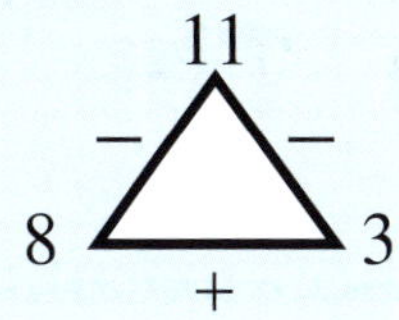

× and ÷ are a pair of inverse operations.

$4 \times 5 = \mathbf{20}$; $20 \div 4 = \mathbf{5}$; $20 \div 5 = \mathbf{4}$

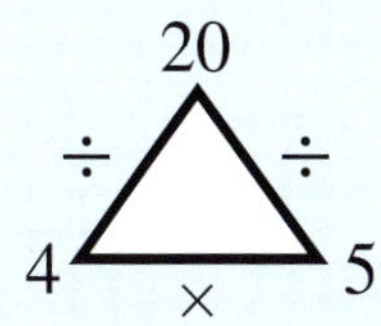

Example: Show adding & subtracting are inverse operations.

$$\begin{array}{r} 34 \\ 43\,+ \\ \hline 77 \\ \hline \end{array} \qquad \begin{array}{r} 77 \\ 34\,- \\ \hline 43 \\ \hline \end{array} \qquad \begin{array}{r} 77 \\ 43\,- \\ \hline 34 \\ \hline \end{array}$$

$34 + 43 = \mathbf{77}$ | $77 - 43 = \mathbf{34}$; $77 - 34 = \mathbf{43}$

Example: Show multiplying & dividing are inverse operations.

$$\begin{array}{r} 8 \\ 9\,\times \\ \hline 72 \\ \hline \end{array} \qquad 9\overline{)72} = 8 \qquad 8\overline{)72} = 9$$

$8 \times 9 = \mathbf{72}$ | $72 \div 8 = \mathbf{9}$; $72 \div 9 = \mathbf{8}$

Exercise 1: 16 Calculate the following: Score ☐

1-2)

$$\begin{array}{r} 32 \\ 93\,+ \\ \hline \square \\ \hline \end{array} \qquad \begin{array}{r} 125 \\ \square\,- \\ \hline 32 \\ \hline \end{array}$$

3-5)

$$\begin{array}{r} 87 \\ \square\,+ \\ \hline 159 \\ \hline \end{array} \qquad \begin{array}{r} \square \\ 72\,- \\ \hline 87 \\ \hline \end{array} \qquad \begin{array}{r} 159 \\ \square\,- \\ \hline 72 \\ \hline \end{array}$$

6-7)

$$\begin{array}{r} 31 \\ 17\,\times \\ \hline \square \\ \hline \end{array} \qquad \begin{array}{r} \square \\ 17\overline{)527} \end{array}$$

8-10)

$$\begin{array}{r} 84 \\ 46\,\times \\ \hline \square \\ \hline \end{array} \qquad \begin{array}{r} \square \\ 84\overline{)3864} \end{array} \qquad \begin{array}{r} \square \\ 46\overline{)3864} \end{array}$$

8. Inverse Problems

All **Inverse Problems** are solved by reversing the operations:

Add ⟷ Subtract **Multiply ⟷ Divide**

a. The Forwards Type

The information in these questions can be dealt with in the order it is given, i.e. in a 'forwards' fashion.

Example: **21** is **7** more than a quarter of this number.

Start here ⟶

− 7 (7 less) **× 4 (4 times)**

(**21**) is **7 more** than a **quarter** of this number.

The sum can be written as: **(21 − 7) × 4 = 56**

Answer: **56**

Exercise 1: 17a Solve the following:

1) **24** is **7** more than **one-fifth** of this number. ______
2) **42** is **12** less than **nine times** this number. ______
3) **15** is **5** more than **one-eighth** of this number. ______
4) **34** is **15** less than **one-seventh** of this number. ______
5) **18** is **9** more than **three times** this number. ______

b. The Backwards Type

The information in these questions is dealt with in reverse order, i.e. in a 'backwards' fashion.

Example: If **4** is added, **7** is subtracted and the answer is **25**.

− 4 (Subtract 4) **+ 7 (Add 7)** ⟵ **Start here**

If **4 is added**, **7 is subtracted** and the answer is (**25**)

The sum can be written as: **(25 + 7) − 4 = 28**

Answer: **28**

Exercise 1: 17b

What is the original number:

Score

6) If **9** is added, **4** is subtracted and the answer is **26**? ____

7) If it is **trebled**, **14** is subtracted and the answer is **43**? ____

8) If **9** is subtracted, **22** is added and the answer is **34**? ____

9) If it is **doubled**, **16** is added and the answer is **18**? ____

10) If **5** is added, then divided by **2** and the answer is **45**? ____

c. Smaller-Larger Type (Add/Subtract)

The inverse operation is indicated by 'smaller' or 'larger'.
If it says it is **smaller** - make it **larger** - **add**.
If it says it is **larger** - make it **smaller** - **subtract**.

Example: **13** is smaller than this number by **29**.

It says it is **smaller** so make it **larger** and **add**.
The sum can be written as: **13 + 29 = 42**

Answer: **42**

Exercise 1: 18a

Solve the following:

1) **60** is larger than this number by **4**. ______

2) **94** is smaller than this number by **29**. ______

3) **86** is larger than this number by **78**. ______

4) **141** is smaller than this number by **52**. ______

5) **292** is larger than this number by **88**. ______

d. Smaller-Larger Type (Multiply/Divide)

The inverse operation in these questions is still indicated by the words 'smaller' or 'larger'. However, if the word **'times'** is included it is a multiply or divide type.
Smaller and **times** means make it **larger** - **multiply**.
Larger and **times** means make it **smaller** - **divide**.

Example: **3** is **6 times** smaller than this number.

It says **smaller** and **times** so make it **larger** - **multiply**.
The sum can be written as: $\mathbf{3 \times 6 = 18}$

Answer: **18**

Exercise 1: 18b

Solve the following:

6) **959** is **7 times** larger than this number. ______

7) **11** is **9 times** smaller than this number. ______

8) **924** is **7 times** larger than this number. ______

9) **4** is **6 times** smaller than this number. ______

10) **30** is **5 times** larger than this number. ______

Score

9. More Number Problems

Exercise 1: 19

Answer the following:

Score

1)
```
 □1 2 8
 5 4□7 −
 ───────
 1□ 4□
```

2) $18\overline{)3078}$

3) **432** × **10,000** = ______

4)
```
 7 4 4 2
     9 4 ×
```

5) Add **67** to **36**, then subtract **7**. Divide by **8**. ______

6) **17** is **11 times** smaller than this number. ______

7)
```
 9 5 9 3
 5 8 0 2 −
```

8)
```
 8 5 7 4
 9 6 0 1 +
```

9) **15** is **19** less than **one-fifth** of this number. ______

10) What number when divided by **12** has an answer of **8** remainder **3**? (Multiply/add.) ______

Chapter Two

NUMBER RELATIONSHIPS

1. Magic Squares

Magic Squares add up to the same amount horizontally and vertically, and sometimes diagonally as well.

Example: Find the value of **A** in this magic square. It adds up to **15** horizontally and vertically (not diagonally).

4		8
A		1
	4	

To find **A**, look for two numbers in the same row or column.
Start with 8 and 1. 8 + 1 = **9**
15 – 9 = 6
Completing the square.
4 + 6 = **10**
15 – 10 = 5
4 + 5 = 9
15 – 9 = 6 **A = 6**

15 ↑	4		8	Start here
A =	**6**		1	↓
15←	**5**	4	**6**	
		←	↓ 15	

Exercise 2: 1 Find the missing amounts:

1) **A** = ______

11		5
A		
	11	4

Adds up to **24** horizontally and vertically only.

2) **A** = ______

25		3
13	**A**	
	9	

Adds up to **46** horizontally and vertically only.

3-4)

A = ______

B = ______

A		15
B		
11	10	18

Adds up to **39** in all directions.

5-6)

A = ______

B = ______

23	16	21
18		**B**
	A	

Adds up to **60** in all directions.

7-8)

A = ______

B = ______

26	16	27
	23	
B		**A**

Adds up to **69** in all directions.

9-10)

A = ______

B = ______

40		20
30		**A**
80	**B**	

Adds up to **150** in all directions.

Score

2. Addition Squares

Addition Squares have two sections. The sums section is grey (numbers to be added) and the answers section is white (answers to addition sums).

Example: Find the value of **A** and **B**.

+	5	**B**
1	6	8
4	**A**	11

There are two missing numbers in this addition square.

+	5	**B**
1	6	8
4	**9**	11

(**Add** the horizontal and vertical numbers to find an addition answer - white squares.)

4 + 5 = **9**

A = 9

+	5	**7**
1	6	8
4	**9**	11

(Reverse the operation to **minus** to find a number to be added - grey squares.)

8 – 1 = **7**

B = 7

Exercise 2: 2 Find the missing amounts: Score

1-2)

A = ______

B = ______

+	8	9
4	**A**	13
5	13	**B**

3-4)

A = ______

B = ______

+	14	17
A	18	21
B	20	23

5-7)

A = ______

B = ______

C = ______

+	**A**	**B**
2	19	21
5	**C**	24

8-10)

A = ______

B = ______

C = ______

+	12	18
A	16	22
B	27	**C**

3. Subtraction Squares

Subtraction Squares work the opposite way to Addition Squares. The sums section is grey (numbers to be subtracted) and the answers section is white (answers to subtraction sums).

Example: Find the value of **A** and **B**.

–	27	**B**
12	15	16
10	**A**	18

There are two missing numbers in this subtraction square.

–	27	**B**
12	15	16
10	**17**	18

(**Subtract** the horizontal and vertical numbers to find a subtraction answer - white squares.)

27 – 10 = **17**

A = 17

–	27	**28**
12	15	16
10	**17**	18

(Reverse the operation to **add** to find a number to be subtracted - grey squares.)

12 + 16 = **28**

B = 28

Exercise 2: 3 Find the missing amounts: **Score**

1-2)

A = ______

B = ______

−	22	18
2	**A**	16
15	7	**B**

3-4)

A = ______

B = ______

−	15	16
A	3	4
B	6	7

5-7)

A = ______

B = ______

C = ______

−	**A**	**B**
8	11	15
6	**C**	17

8-10)

A = ______

B = ______

C = ______

−	17	20
A	12	15
B	15	**C**

4. Multiplication Squares

Multiplication Squares have two sections. The sums section is grey (numbers to be multiplied) and the answers section is white (answers to multiplication sums).

Example:

Find the value of **A** and **B**.

×	4	8	10
2	8	16	20
6	24	**A**	60
B	32	64	80

×	4	8	10
2	8	16	20
6	24	**48**	60
8	32	64	80

(**Multiply** the horizontal and vertical grey numbers to find an answer - white squares.)

$6 \times 8 =$ **48**

A = 48

(Reverse the operation by **dividing** to find a multiplier for one of the sums - grey squares.)

$32 \div 4 =$ **8**

B = 8

Exercise 2: 4 Find the missing amounts: **Score**

1-2)
A = ______
B = ______

×	3	7	11
5	15	35	55
6	18	**A**	66
B	24	56	88

3-4)
A = ______
B = ______

×	5	8	12
2	10	16	**A**
B	30	48	72
10	50	80	120

5-7)
A = ______
B = ______
C = ______

×	6	9	**A**
3	**B**	27	33
4	24	36	44
12	72	**C**	121

8-10)
A = ______
B = ______
C = ______

×	**A**	5	9
4	16	**B**	36
6	24	30	54
C	28	35	63

5. Division Squares

Division Squares work the opposite way to Multiplication Squares. The sums section is grey (numbers to be divided) and the answers section is white (answers to division sums).

Example:

Find the value of **A** and **B**.

÷	**B**	56	32
2	12	28	16
8	3	**A**	4
4	6	14	8

÷	**24**	56	32
2	12	28	16
8	3	**7**	4
4	6	14	8

$56 \div 8 = \mathbf{7}$

A = 7

$4 \times 6 = \mathbf{24}$

B = 24

(**Divide** the horizontal and vertical grey numbers to find an answer - white squares.)
(Reverse the operation to **multiplication** to find a dividend for one of the sums - grey squares.)

Exercise 2: 5 Find the missing amounts: **Score**

1-2)
A = ______
B = ______

÷	30	60	18
3	10	20	6
2	15	**A**	9
B	5	10	3

3-4)
A = ______
B = ______

÷	24	56	32
2	12	28	**A**
B	3	7	4
4	6	14	8

5-7)
A = ______
B = ______
C = ______

÷	72	48	**A**
8	**B**	6	3
6	12	8	4
12	6	**C**	2

8-10)
A = ______
B = ______
C = ______

÷	**A**	72	108
9	4	**B**	12
3	12	24	36
C	3	6	9

6. Approximating Numbers

Approximate means 'near enough'. It is a rough guide.
Example: **6 × 52** when calculated comes to **312** exactly.
For 'easy numbers', make the **52** into **50**.
6 × 50 would give an approximate answer of **300**.

Round numbers give a 'near enough' answer by taking the number up or down to the nearest **power of ten**.

To the nearest 10.	**592** would be	→ **590**
To the nearest 100.	**703** would be	→ **700**
To the nearest 1,000.	**9,900** would be	→ **10,000**

A number of **5 or more rounds up**; **4 or less rounds down**. Example: **95** would round up to **100** (nearest ten).

Exercise 2: 6 Round these numbers to the:

Score

Nearest 10.	Nearest 100.	Nearest 1,000.
1) **16** _____	3) **212** _____	5) **8,087** _____
2) **963** _____	4) **442** _____	6) **7,059** _____

Approximate these sums (≈ means 'nearly equal to'):

7) **56** + **21** ≈ _____ 8) **3** × **79** ≈ _____

9) **758** – **137** ≈ _____ 10) **721** ÷ **78** ≈ _____

7. Odd and Even Numbers

An **Even Number** is any number that can be divided by **2** exactly.

Even numbers - **0, 2**, **4**, **6**, **8**, **10**, **12**, **14**, **16**, **18**, etc.

All even numbers end with **0**, **2**, **4**, **6** or **8**.

An **Odd Number** is any number that cannot be divided by **2**.

Odd numbers - **1**, **3**, **5**, **7**, **9**, **11**, **13**, **15**, **17**, **19**, etc.

All odd numbers end with **1**, **3**, **5**, **7** or **9**.

Exercise 2: 7 Write odd or even by each number:

1) **32** _____ 2) **97** _____ 3) **898** _____ 4) **369** _____

5) **440** _____ 6) **93** _____ 7) **976** _____ 8) **38** _____

9) List the numbers from above that are divisible by **2**:

_____ _____ _____ _____ _____

10) **8,496** does/does not divide by **2** - underline.

Score

8. Squares

a. Square Numbers

A **Square Number** is a number multiplied by itself.
It is based on the shape of a square.

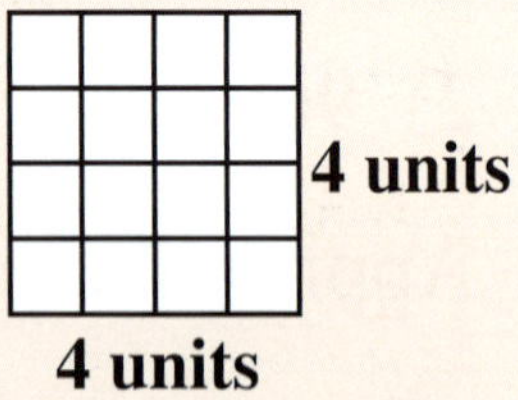

Example: What is $\mathbf{4^2}$?

The symbol ^{2} means 'to the power of 2'.
$\mathbf{4^2}$ means $\mathbf{4 \times 4}$ which is **16**.

$\mathbf{4^2 = 4 \times 4 = 16}$

Answer: **16**

Exercise 2: 8 Write the square of the following:

1) $\mathbf{5^2}$ = ____ 2) $\mathbf{6^2}$ = ____ 3) $\mathbf{8^2}$ = ____

4) $\mathbf{10^2}$ = ____ 5) $\mathbf{12^2}$ = ____ 6) $\mathbf{13^2}$ = ____

7) $\mathbf{14^2}$ = _____ 8) $\mathbf{15^2}$ = _____

9) $\mathbf{20^2}$ = _____ 10) $\mathbf{24^2}$ = _____

Score

b. Square Roots

A **Square Root** is the number a square has come from.

Example: What is the square root of **16**? $\mathbf{4^2 = 4 \times 4 = 16}$

Hence **4** is the square root of **16**. It is the inverse operation.

Square ⟷ Square Root Square root is written $\sqrt{\ }$

Answer: $\sqrt{\mathbf{16}}$ = **4** (The square root of **16** is **4**.)

Exercise 2: 9 Write the square roots of the following:

1) $\sqrt{\mathbf{100}}$ = _____ 2) $\sqrt{\mathbf{36}}$ = _____

3) $\sqrt{\mathbf{64}}$ = _____ 4) $\sqrt{\mathbf{4}}$ = _____

5) $\sqrt{\mathbf{9}}$ = _____ 6) $\sqrt{\mathbf{121}}$ = _____

7) $\sqrt{144}$ = ______ 8) $\sqrt{25}$ = ______

9) $\sqrt{49}$ = ______ 10) $\sqrt{81}$ = ______

Be familiar with square numbers.

Root	Square	Root	Square	Root	Square	Root	Square
1	1	**6**	36	**11**	121	**16**	256
2	4	**7**	49	**12**	144	**17**	289
3	9	**8**	64	**13**	169	**18**	324
4	16	**9**	81	**14**	196	**19**	361
5	25	**10**	100	**15**	225	**20**	400

9. Cubes

a. Cube Numbers

A **Cube Number** is a number multiplied by itself twice. It is based on the shape of a cube.

Example: What is 9^3?

9 cubed (9^3) = $\mathbf{9 \times \overset{81}{9} \times \overset{729}{9} = 729}$

To cube means to raise a number 'to the power of 3'.

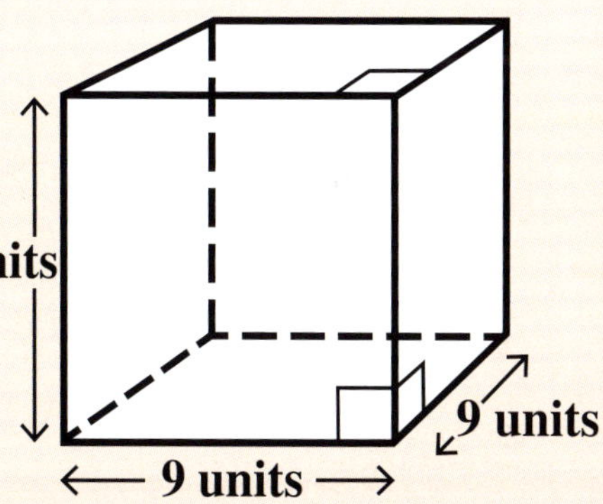

Answer: **729**

Exercise 2: 10 Write the cubes of the following:

1) 5^3 = ______ 2) 11^3 = ______

3) 7^3 = ______ 4) 6^3 = ______

5) 10^3 = ______ 6) 2^3 = ______

7) 4^3 = ______ 8) 3^3 = ______

9) 8^3 = ______ 10) 12^3 = ______

10. Prime Numbers

A **Prime Number** has only two factors (**itself** and **1**). It is a number which will not divide by anything else but **itself** and **1**.

- The first ten prime numbers are:

  2, **3**, **5**, **7**, **11**, **13**, **17**, **19**, **23** and **29**

- All prime numbers, except **2**, are odd.
- **1** is not a prime number (it has only one factor - itself).
- Prime numbers do not appear in any other times tables.
- Prime numbers usually end in **1**, **3**, **7** or **9**.

Example: What are the prime numbers between **1** and **9**?

1, **2**, **3**, 4, **5**, 6, **7**, 8, 9

2, **3**, **5** and **7** are prime numbers.

Factors (1, 2) (1, 3) (1, 5) (1, 7)

Each number is only divisible by **itself** and **1**.

Answer: **2**, **3**, **5** and **7**

Exercise 2: 11 Write whether the following numbers are prime or not prime:

Score

1) **11** is ______________ 2) **28** is ______________

3) **23** is ______________ 4) **22** is ______________

5) **33** is ______________ 6) **43** is ______________

7) **46** is ______________ 8) **49** is ______________

9) **40** is ______________ 10) **37** is ______________

11. Rectangular Numbers

Rectangular Numbers are based on the times tables. Every times tables calculation can be represented as a rectangle or a square.

- All even numbers except **2** are rectangular.
- Prime numbers are never rectangular.
- The first six rectangular numbers are: **4**, **6**, **8**, **9**, **10**, **12**
- Square numbers are also classed as rectangular numbers.

Example: Is **6** a rectangular number?

As shown by the grid, **6** is a rectangular number because $\mathbf{3 \times 2 = 6}$ forms a rectangle.

$\mathbf{3 \times 2 = 6}$

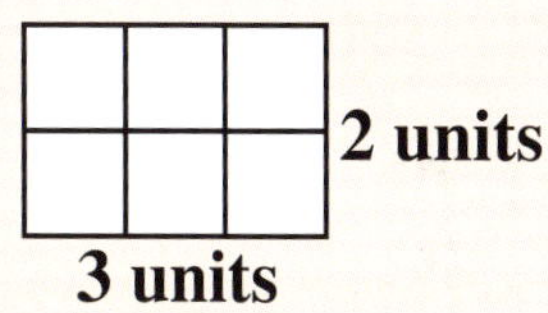

Answer: **6** is a rectangular number.

Exercise 2: 12 Are the following numbers rectangular?

1)	**23**	yes/no	2)	**19**	yes/no
3)	**14**	yes/no	4)	**43**	yes/no
5)	**46**	yes/no	6)	**37**	yes/no

What rectangular numbers do the following make?

7)	**9** and **2** = ____	8)	**5** and **2** = ____
9)	**7** and **5** = ____	10)	**7** and **3** = ____

12. Triangular Numbers

Triangular Numbers are based on a triangular pattern.

Example: What are the first 4 triangular numbers?

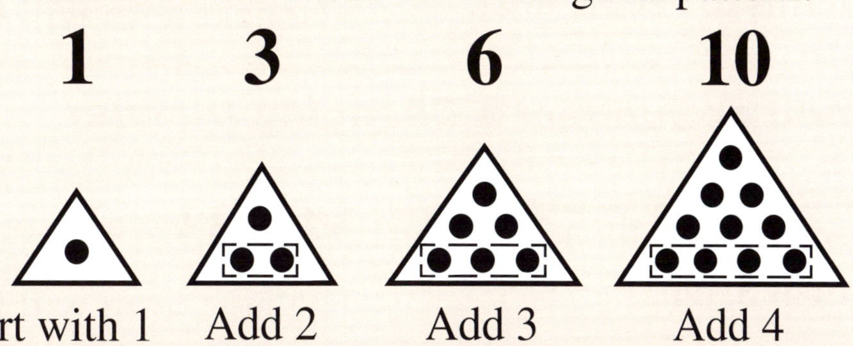

For the fifth triangular number add **5** and so on.

$$\mathbf{1}\ ^{+2}\ \ \mathbf{3}\ ^{+3}\ \ \mathbf{6}\ ^{+4}\ \ \mathbf{10}\ ^{+5}\ \ \mathbf{15}\ ^{+6}\ \ \text{etc.}$$

Exercise 2: 13

Write the following triangular numbers:

Score

1) The **6th** is _____ .
2) The **10th** is _____ .
3) The **8th** is _____ .
4) The **7th** is _____ .
5) The **5th** is _____ .
6) The **9th** is _____ .

Add two triangular numbers to make the following:

7) **36** = ____ + ____
8) **42** = ____ + ____
9) **7** = ____ + ____
10) **18** = ____ + ____

13. Number Sequences

Number Sequences are series of numbers connected by rules, which create patterns.

Add or Subtract the Same Number

Example 1:

Add **2** to the previous number.

$$\mathbf{4,}\ ^{+2}\ \mathbf{6,}\ ^{+2}\ \mathbf{8,}\ ^{+2}\ \mathbf{10,}\ ^{+2}\ \mathbf{12,}\ ^{+2}\ \mathbf{14}$$

The next term will be **16**.

Add the Previous Two Terms

Example 2:

Add the two previous terms to get the next.

$$\mathbf{1,}\ \ \mathbf{3,}\ ^{1+3}\ \mathbf{4,}\ ^{3+4}\ \mathbf{7,}\ ^{4+7}\ \mathbf{11,}\ ^{7+11}\ \mathbf{18}$$

The next term will be **29**.

Add or Subtract a Changing Number

Example 3:

Subtract **1**, then **2**, then **3**, etc.

$$\mathbf{34,}\ ^{-1}\ \mathbf{33,}\ ^{-2}\ \mathbf{31,}\ ^{-3}\ \mathbf{28,}\ ^{-4}\ \mathbf{24}$$

The next term will be **19**.

Multiply or Divide by the Same Number

Example 4:

Multiply the previous number by **2**.

6, $\overset{\times 2}{}$ **12,** $\overset{\times 2}{}$ **24,** $\overset{\times 2}{}$ **48,** $\overset{\times 2}{}$ **96**

The next term will be **192**.

Multiply or Divide by a Changing Number

Example 5:

Divide by **5**, then by **4**, then by **5**, etc.

2,000, $\overset{\div 5}{}$ **400,** $\overset{\div 4}{}$ **100,** $\overset{\div 5}{}$ **20**

The next term will be **5**.

Number sequences come in many forms - watch out for:

- Combined operations, e.g. multiply by **3**, then add **2**, etc.
- Square and cube numbers, e.g. **4**, **9**, **16**, **25**, **36**, etc.

Exercise 2: 14a Write in the missing numbers:

1) **5,000, 1,000, 200,** __ , __
2) **51, 46, 41,** __ , __
3) **3, 7, 10, 17,** __ , __
4) **2, 4, 8,** __ , **32,** __
5) **6, 8, 13, 15,** __ , __
6) **9, 10, 5, 6, 3,** __ , __

Number sequences can be made using diagrams.

Example: | What sequence does this pattern make? |

Count the cubes.

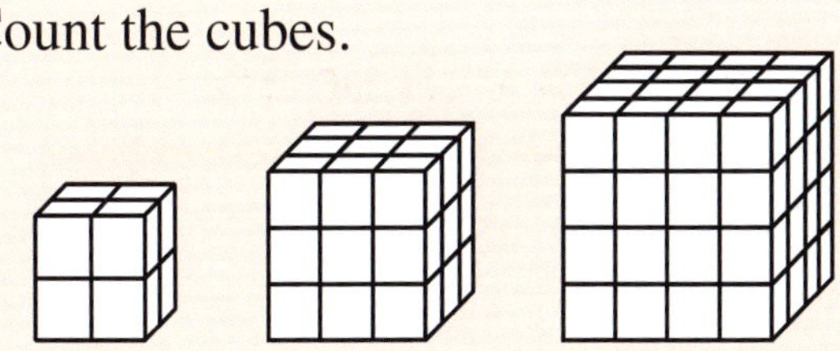

8 27 64

The pattern is 8, 27, 64

The next three numbers are:

8, 27, 64, **125, 216, 343**

Exercise 2: 14b Write the next two numbers:

Score

7)  __ , __

8)  __ , __

9)  __ , __

10) 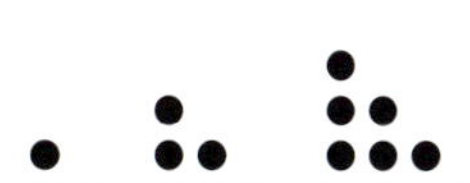 __ , __

14. Number Lines

Numbers are sometimes shown on a **Number Line**. Missing numbers are found by examining the given sequence.

Example: What are the missing numbers on this number line?

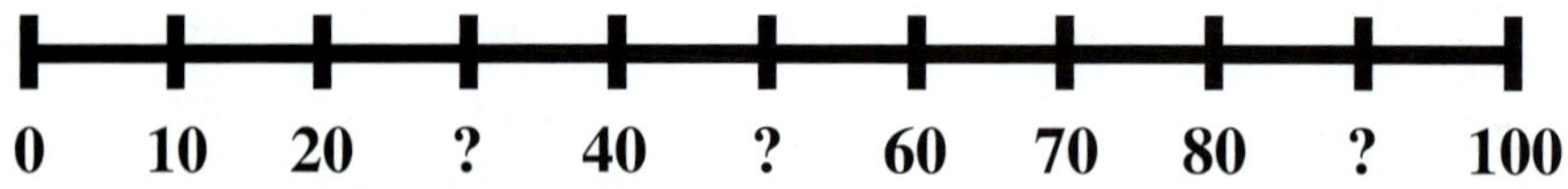

The sequence rises by **10** each time.

Answer: **30**, **50** and **90**

Exercise 2: 15 What are the missing numbers?

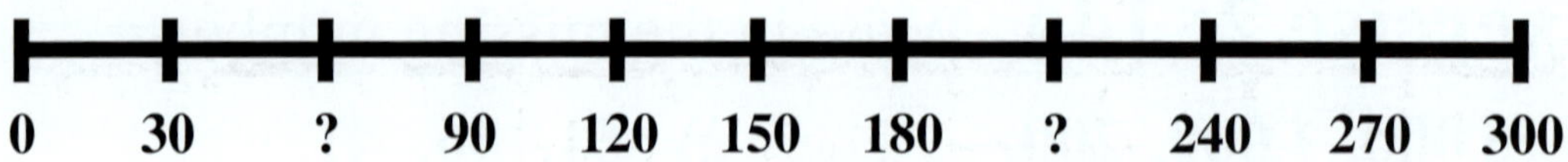

1-2) The missing numbers are: _____ _____

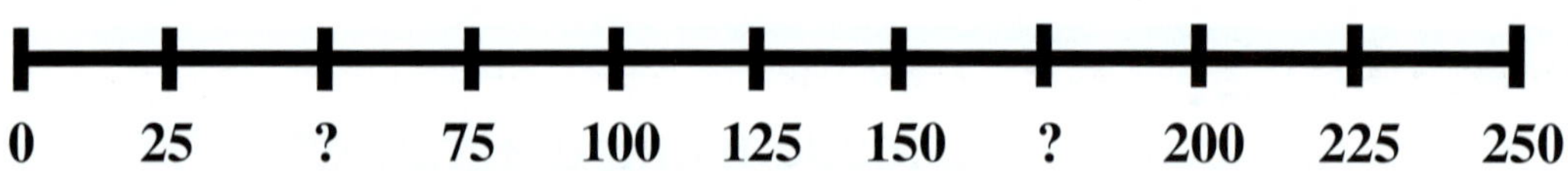

3-4) The missing numbers are: _____ _____

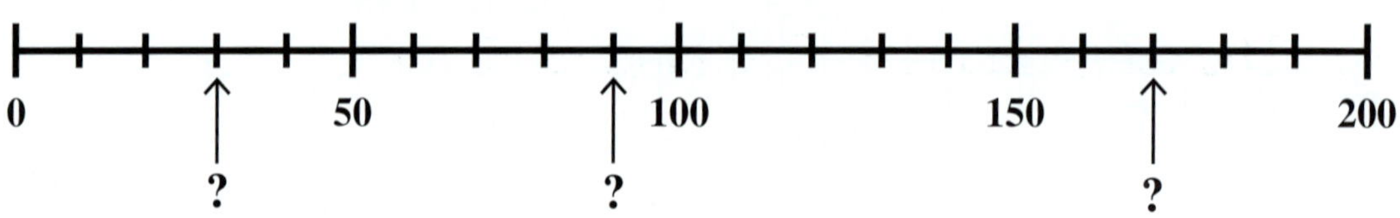

5-7) The missing numbers are: _____ _____ _____

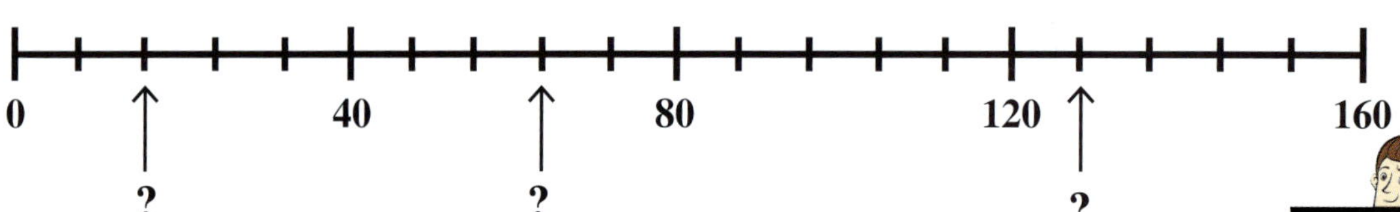

8-10) The missing numbers are: _____ _____ _____

Score

15. Positive & Negative Numbers

Whole numbers (**integers**) can be **Positive** or **Negative**. Positive and negative numbers are also known as Directed Numbers and can be represented on a **number line** (known as an **integer line** if it shows whole numbers only).

Positive (+ plus numbers) **2**, **20**, **56**
Negative (– minus numbers) **-19**, **-41**, **-60**

The signs (+ & –) show the **direction** of the numbers.

Remember to count the gaps on the integer line and not the digits, including the gaps either side of the zero.

Example: What is the gap between **-4** and **2**?

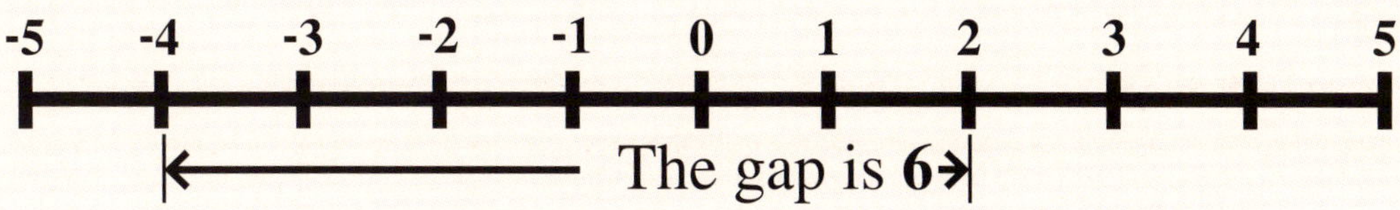

Answer: **6**

Exercise 2: 16a Use the integer line for the following.

Write the gap between: 1) **-3** and **5**. ____ 2) **1** and **-4**. ____

3) On a winter evening the temperature was **6°C**. It fell by **10°C**. What is the new temperature? ____

4) The temperature in Scotland fell by **3°C** overnight. It started out as **2°C**. What was the new temperature by morning? ____

5) What is the difference in temperature between **-5°C** and **6°C**? ____

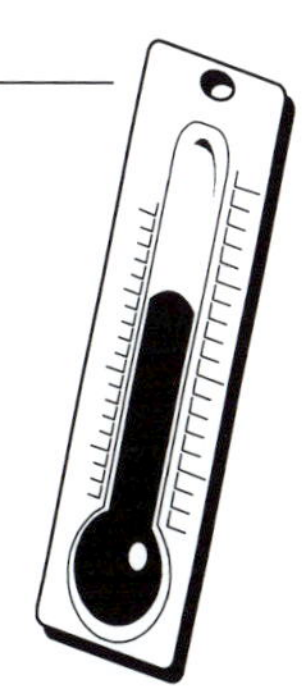

Numbers to the **right** are **bigger** and to the **left** are **smaller**.

⟵ (smaller than) < > (bigger than) ⟶

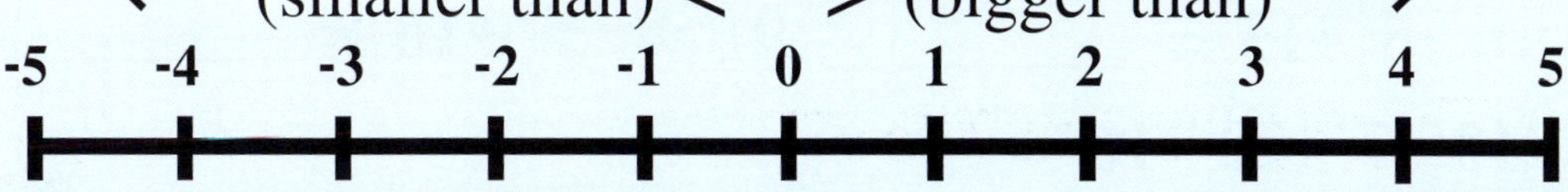

The signs < (smaller than) and > (bigger than) show the relationship between two numbers.

An easy rule: 'The mouth of the crocodile (open end) always swallows the biggest number'.

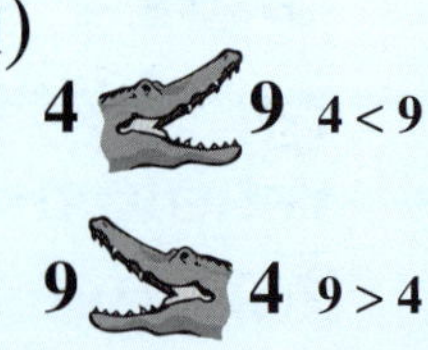

Examples: Use < or > between these numbers.

1 > -2   **-5 < 5**   **-1 > -4**   **-3 < 0**

Exercise 2: 16b Answer the following:

6) Put the signs > or < between these pairs of numbers:
a) **-1**   **5**   b) **-10**   **4**   c) **1**   **-4**

7) Put these numbers in order **-1**, **2**, **-4**, **6**, **9**, **-9**, **7**
lowest first: ___ ___ ___ ___ ___ ___ ___

Adding and Subtracting Directed Numbers

2 rules: • Always start counting at zero.
• Count **right** for positive/**left** for negative numbers.

Example: Work out **+3 -4 -1**   **+3 -4 -1 = 0**

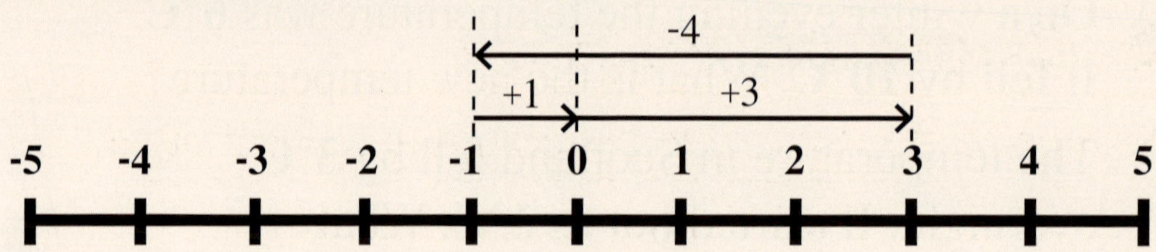

Answer: **0**

Exercise 2: 16c Calculate the following: **Score**

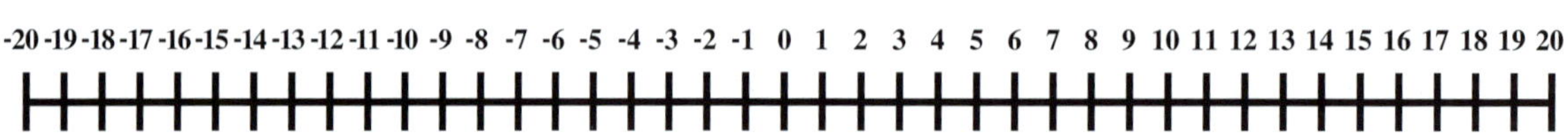

8) **+6 -5 +15** = ______   9) **-8 -6 +16** = ______

10) **-10 -7 +20 -18** = ______

16. Factors
a. What is a Factor?

Factors are numbers that divide exactly into one number (or more) without remainders.

Example: What are the factors of **72**?

To find the factors of **72**, multiply **1** by **72** then **2** by **36**, etc.

1 × **72**; **2** × **36**; **3** × **24**; **4** × **18**; **6** × **12**; **8** × **9**

72 cannot be divided by **7** and **9** × **8** is the same as **8** × **9**.

Therefore, these are all the numbers that divide into **72**.

Answer: **1, 2, 3, 4, 6, 8, 9, 12, 18, 24, 36, 72**

Exercise 2: 17 Find the factors of the following numbers:

Score

1) **20** ______________ 2) **12** ______________

3) **22** ______________ 4) **28** ______________

5) **55** ______________ 6) **48** ______________

7) **84** ______________ 8) **85** ______________

9) **95** ______________ 10) **51** ______________

b. Common Factors

Numbers often share factors common to each other.

Example: Give the common factors of **21** and **24**.

21 **1**, **3**, 7, 21

24 **1**, 2, **3**, 4, 6, 8, 12, 24

The common factors of **21** and **24** are **1** and **3**.

Exercise 2: 18a Underline the common factors of:

1) **15** and **24** (**2**, **3**, **4**, **6**) 2) **21** and **42** (**1**, **2**, **3**, **4**, **7**, **21**)

3) **28** and **49** (**3**, **6**, **7**, **14**) 4) **15** and **45** (**2**, **3**, **5**, **8**, **15**)

c. Highest Common Factors (HCF)

A **Highest Common Factor** (HCF) is the highest number that divides exactly into two (or more) other numbers.

Example: What is the HCF of **15**, **39** and **48**?

15 - 1, **3**, 5, 15
39 - 1, **3**, 13, 39
48 - 1, 2, **3**, 4, 6, 8, 12, 16, 24, 48

The highest common factor (HCF) is **3**.

Exercise 2: 18b Find the HCF of the following:

Score

5) **35** and **14** ______

6) **39** and **78** ______

7) **50**, **75** and **45** ______

8) **22**, **33** and **88** ______

9) **12** and **48** ______

10) **42**, **28** and **70** ______

d. Prime Factors

A **Prime Factor** is a prime number that divides into another number exactly.

Example: Express the prime factors of **20**.

Prime factors can be found by using a factor tree. This can be done by listing the pairs of factors. Successive branches can be created until all the factors are shown as prime numbers.

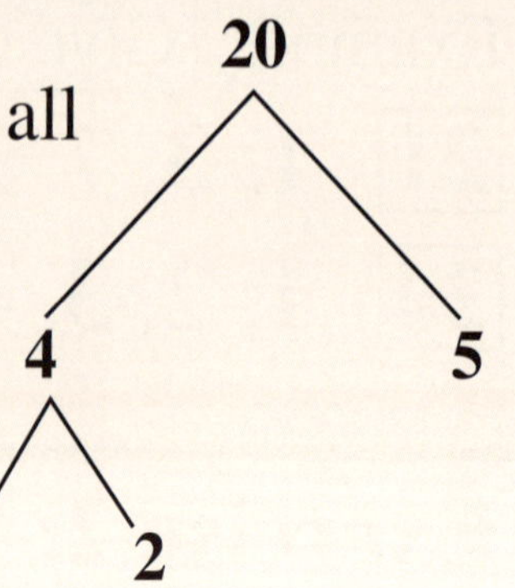

2 and **5** are both prime factors of **20** because they are prime numbers and divide into **20**.

20 is expressed as a product of its prime factors by using indices.

$2 \times 2 \times 5$

$2^2 \times 5 = 20$

Exercise 2: 19 Write the prime factors of the following:

1) **14**

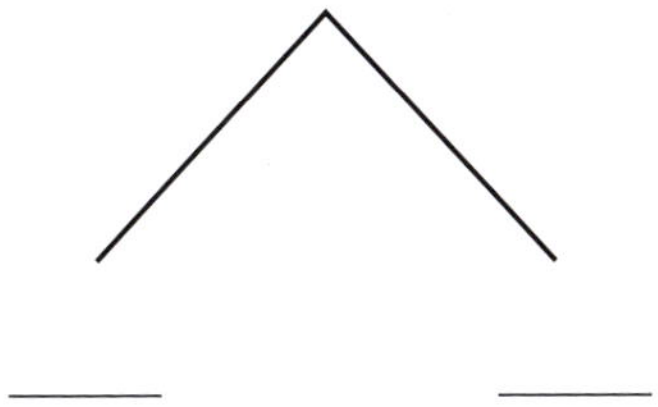

2) **38**

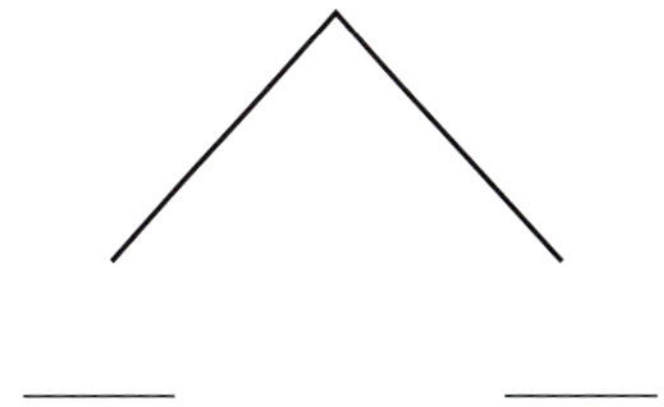

3) **36**

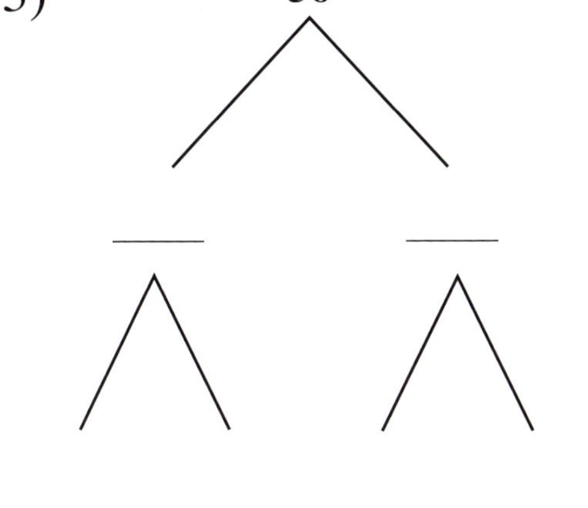

4) **72**

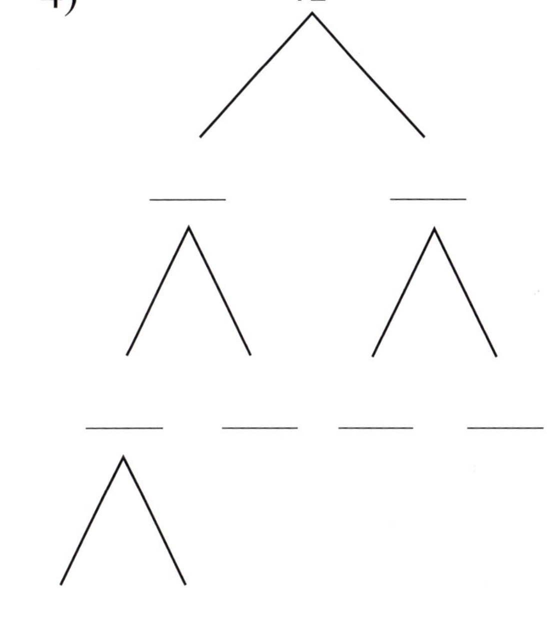

5) **68**

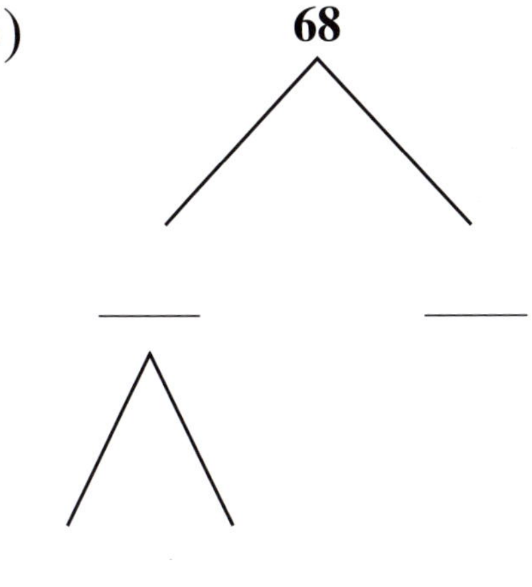

6) **66**

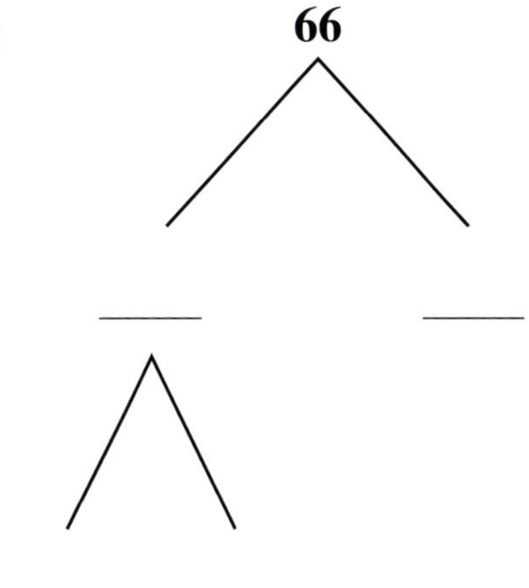

Write the missing prime factor:

7) 2^3 × ____ = **24** 8) 2^2 × ____ = **100**

9) 2^2 × ____ = **44** 10) 3^2 × ____ = **63**

17. Multiples

a. What is a Multiple?

A **Multiple** is any number in the times table of a number. For example, multiples of **10** would be: **10**, **20**, **30**, **40**, etc.

Exercise 2: 20 Write the next five multiples:

1) **9** ___ ___ ___ ___ ___ 2) **13** ___ ___ ___ ___ ___

3) **14** ___ ___ ___ ___ ___ 4) **3** ___ ___ ___ ___ ___

5) **12** ___ ___ ___ ___ ___ 6) **7** ___ ___ ___ ___ ___

7) **15** ___ ___ ___ ___ ___ 8) **2** ___ ___ ___ ___ ___

9) **8** ___ ___ ___ ___ ___ 10) **19** ___ ___ ___ ___ ___

b. Common Multiples

Numbers often share multiples common to each other.

Example: Give two common multiples of **3** and **9**.

3 3, 6, **9**, 12, 15, **18**

9 **9**, **18**, 27, 36

9 and **18** are common multiples as both numbers divide by **3** and **9**.

Exercise 2: 21a Underline the common multiples of:

1) **4** and **6** (**12**, **16**, **18**, **24**, **30**) 2) **6** and **10** (**30**, **40**, **60**, **72**)

3) **11** and **2** (**12**, **22**, **24**, **44**) 4) **8** and **12** (**12**, **24**, **32**, **48**)

c. Lowest Common Multiples (LCM)

The **Lowest (Least) Common Multiple** of two (or more) numbers is the smallest possible number into which all of them will divide.

Example: Give the LCM of **3**, **5** and **6**.

The lowest number that	**3**	3, 6, 9, 12, 15, 18, 21, 24, 27, **30**
all three of these numbers	**5**	10, 15, 20, 25, **30**
will divide into is **30**.	**6**	12, 18, 24, **30**

Written questions also use LCM.

Example: What is the smallest number of peaches that can be arranged in baskets of either **2**, **4** or **5**?

Answer: **20** peaches

Exercise 2: 21b What is the LCM of:

Score

5) **4** and **7** ___ 6) **7** and **9** ___ 7) **3**, **4** and **6** ___

8) **3** and **8** ___ 9) **4**, **8** and **12** ___ 10) **4** and **8** ___

18. Applied Number Problems

Number Problems require the use of: + − × ÷

Example: A forest has **15** apple trees, **three times** as many orange trees and **four times** as many pear trees. How many trees are there?

15 apple trees + **45** orange trees ($3 \times 15 =$) + **60** pear trees ($4 \times 15 =$) = **120** trees

Answer: **120**

Exercise 2: 22 Calculate the following:

1) A crate holds 30 boxes of pens. Each box has 50 pens in. How many pens does the crate hold? ________ (Multiply.)

2) There are **200** children and **14** teachers going on a school trip. If each coach can take **42** people, how many coaches will be needed? ________ (Add and divide.)

3) A train going from Hull to York has **three** carriages with **90** seats each. There are **28** seats empty in each carriage. How many seats are occupied? ________ (Multiply and subtract.)

4) A darts player hits triple **19** with his first dart, single **17** with his second and double **18** with his third. What is his total score? ________ (Multiply and add.)

5) There are **seven** months with **31** days. What is the total number of days in these months? ________ (Multiply.)

6) Akhil counts the number of vehicles he sees drive past his house during the day. He sees **26** cars, **13** vans and **8** motorcycles. How many vehicles does he see altogether? ________ (Add.)

7) A teacher sets **27** pages of homework. **One** student doesn't finish the last **9** pages. How many pages are completed? ________ (Subtract.)

8) There are **30** questions in a test. **5** children sit the test and between them get **12** wrong answers. How many questions did they get correct? ________ (Multiply and subtract.)

9) A bus with **six** passengers leaves the station. At the first stop, **2** passengers get off and **3** get on. At the second stop, **seven** passengers get off and **twelve** passengers get on. At the third stop, no one gets off and **two** people get on. How many people are now on the bus? ________ (Add and subtract.)

10) A CD holds **12** songs. Sophia buys **8** CDs. How many songs are there in total? ________ (Multiply.)

Score

19. Roman Numerals

Roman Numerals are a useful alternative counting system. They are based on the symbols below:

I = 1, **V** = 5, **X** = 10, **L** = 50,
C = 100, **D** = 500, **M** = 1,000

These symbols are combined to represent numbers. The numbers from **1** to **10** are listed below:

I	II	III	IV	V	VI	VII	VIII	IX	X
1	2	3	4	5	6	7	8	9	10

When a symbol appears after a larger symbol it is added.
When a symbol appears before a larger symbol it is subtracted.
4 and **9** are made by subtracting from **5** and **10**.

−1 ↘ 5 ↙	−1 ↘ 10 ↙	10 ↘ −1 ↘ 5 ↙	−10 ↘ 50 ↙
IV	**IX**	**XIV**	**XL**
5 – 1 = **4**	10 – 1 = **9**	10 + 5 – 1 = **14**	50 – 10 = **40**

Example: Show how **1,400**, **2,450** and **2,474** are written.

1000 ↓ M ¦ 400 ↓ CD	2000 ↓ MM ¦ 400 ↓ CD ¦ 50 ↓ L	2000 ↓ MM ¦ 400 ↓ CD ¦ 70 ↓ LXX ¦ 4 ↓ IV
MCD	**MMCDL**	**MMCDLXXIV**
1,400	**2,450**	**2,474**

Exercise 2: 23 Convert to denary: **Score** 

1) **XVIII** ________ 2) **CDLXXIX** ________
3) **DCCLXXXV** ________ 4) **CCCLVII** ________
5) **MVII** ________ 6) **MCMLXXI** ________
7) **MCDLV** ________ 8) **MMDCCCXCIV** ________
9) **MMMDCCCXXV** ________ 10) **CMLXXV** ________

Exercise 2: 24 Convert to Roman numerals:

1) **56** ______ 2) **13** ______

3) **406** ______ 4) **41** ______

5) **735** ______ 6) **871** ______

7) **1,214** ______ 8) **1,308** ______

9) **3,770** ______

10) **1,542** ______

Score

20. Number Relationship Problems

Exercise 2: 25 Answer the following:

Score

1) a) **A** = ____ **B** = ____

18	13	17
15	**B**	
A		14

Adds up to **48** in all directions.

b) **A** = ____ **B** = ____

45	37	44
B		**A**
		39

Adds up to **126** in all directions.

2) a) $\mathbf{15^2}$ = ______ b) $\mathbf{4^3}$ = ______ c) $\mathbf{9^3}$ = ______

d) What is the square root of **100**? ______

3) a) Write the first five triangular numbers.

____ ____ ____ ____ ____

b) Which of these numbers are rectangular? __ __ __

c) Add the prime numbers between **4** and **15**. ______

d) What rectangular number does this dot pattern represent? ____

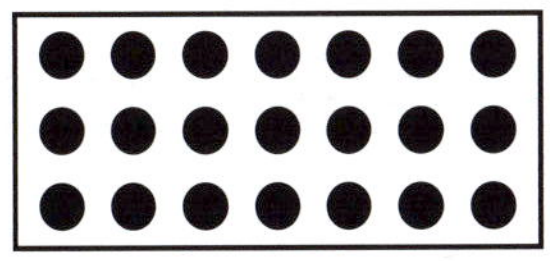

4) Write the next two numbers in the series:

a) **1**, **8**, **27**, **64**, ___ , ___ b) **16**, **32**, ___ , **64**, ___

5) a) What is the gap between **-9** and **8**? _____

Work out: b) **-3** **+3** **-2** _____ c) **+5** **-4** **+3** _____

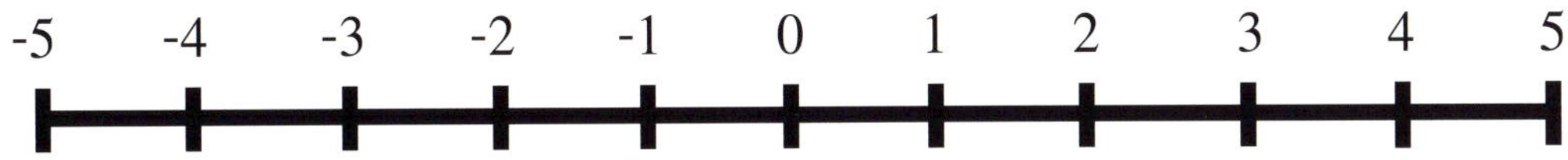

6) a) Write all the factors of **28**. __________________

b) What is the highest common factor (HCF) of: **48**, **72** and **84**? _______

c) What are the prime factors of **36**? _________

d) $\mathbf{3^2}$ is a prime factor of **18**. What is the other prime factor? _______

7) What is the lowest common multiple (LCM) of:

a) **6**, **8** and **9**? ____ b) **3**, **12** and **5**? ____

c) **11**, **6** and **2**? ____

8) How many seats are there in an aeroplane that has **34** rows of **3** seats each side of the centre aisle? _____

9) A box holds **8** packs of marbles. Each pack holds **16** marbles. How many marbles are in a box? _____

10) How many bottles of lemonade would be needed to fill **134** glasses if each bottle holds **7** glasses? _____

Chapter Three
DECIMALS
1. Tens Number System

The **Tens Number System** can be extended to numbers smaller than a unit, such as tenths, hundredths, thousandths, etc. These are called **Decimals**.

Numbers can be displayed on a **Decimal Table** (shown below) to help determine place value.

Whole number ⟵ ⟶ Less than a whole one

TH	H	T	U	t	h	th
3	0	1	8 •	4	2	5

The **Decimal Point** separates the whole numbers from the decimals.

Key
TH - Thousands
H - Hundreds
T - Tens
U - Units
t - tenths
h - hundredths
th - thousandths

This number has been written to three **Decimal Places**.

3 0 1 8 . **4 2 5**

Whole number | **4** tenths, **2** hundredths, **5** thousandths

Study the table to see how units, tenths, hundredths and thousandths are written.

Whole number ⟵ ⟶ **Less than a whole one**

	U	t	h	th
One unit →	1 •			
One tenth →	0 •	1		
One hundredth →	0 •	0	1	
One thousandth →	0 •	0	0	1

Going from **left** to **right** each column is **ten times** smaller than the previous.

e.g.

→ $1 \div 10 = \mathbf{\frac{1}{10}}$

→ $\frac{1}{10} \div 10 = \mathbf{\frac{1}{100}}$

→ $\frac{1}{100} \div 10 = \mathbf{\frac{1}{1000}}$

This diagram compares the size of a unit, a tenth and a hundredth.

One unit One tenth One hundredth

It is written as: **1.11**

It could be expressed as: **1 unit**, **1 tenth** and **1 hundredth**
or **11 tenths** and **1 hundredth**
or **1 unit** and **11 hundredths**
or **111 hundredths**

2. Place Value

a. Whole Numbers as Decimals

All **Whole Numbers** can be expressed as a **Decimal**.

Example: Express **2** and **13** as decimals.

Put a decimal point after the number, followed by a zero.

Answer: **2.0** and **13.0**

Exercise 3: 1 Express these whole numbers:

With a decimal point.

1) **8** ________
2) **34** ________
3) **69** ________
4) **504** ________
5) **9,590** ________

Without a decimal point.

6) **5.0** ________
7) **84.0** ________
8) **37.0** ________
9) **765.0** ________
10) **7,958.0** ________

Score

b. The Decimal Table

Decimals can be placed on the decimal table for clarity.

Example: Place **5,689.758** on the decimal table.

Use the decimal point to correctly place the number.

TH	H	T	U	t	h	th
5	6	8	9 •	7	5	8

Exercise 3: 2 Put these numbers on the decimal table:

Score

1) **40.28**

2) **1.267**

TH	H	T	U	t	h	th
___	___	___	___ •	___	___	___
___	___	___	___ •	___	___	___

3) **525.7**

4) **20.64**

5) **6,243.906**

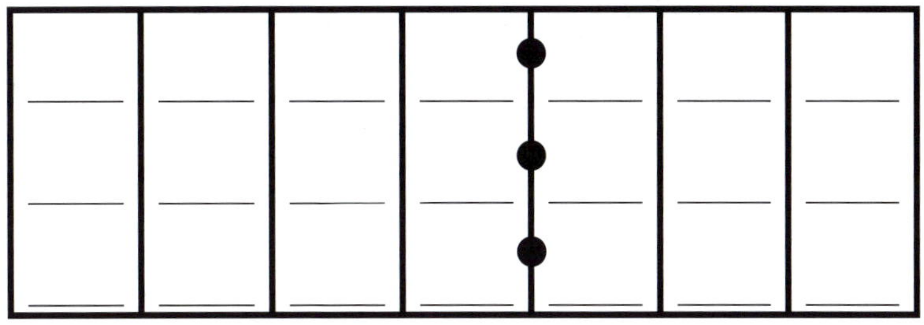

Draw a decimal table and place these numbers on it.

6) **7.3** 7) **6.42** 8) **0.256** 9) **541.71** 10) **4,539.53**

c. Value of Decimals

The **Value of a Decimal Digit** is indicated by its position in the number.

Example: What is the value of the **8** in the number **3.798**?

3.79**8**

8 thousandths

9 hundredths

7 tenths

Whole number

Answer: **8 thousandths**

Exercise 3: 3 Write the value of the following:

Score

1) The **5** in **7.507** = ____________________

2) The **8** in **0.78** = ____________________

3) The **6** in **2.067** = ____________________

4) The **3** in **3.90** = ____________________

5) The **9** in **95.018** = ____________________

6) The **1** in **6.184** = ____________________

Underline the required value in the following:

7) Thousandths in **0.738** 8) Units in **5.06**

9) Hundredths in **7.18** 10) Tenths in **7.563**

d. Expressing Decimal Values

The value of a decimal can be expressed as follows:

Example: Show **9.159** on the decimal table.

Whole number ⟵ ¦ ⟶ Less than a whole one

U	t	h	th
9	• **1**	**5**	**9**

It can be expressed as: **9 units**, **1 tenth**, **5 hundredths**, **9 thousandths.**

or **9 units**, **1 tenth**, **59 thousandths.**

or **9 units**, **159 thousandths.**

or **9,159 thousandths.**

Note that these are only a few examples of the ways the number can be expressed.

Exercise 3: 4 Write the value of the following:

1) **8.981** in thousandths = ______________________

2) **5.75** in hundredths = ______________________

3) **78.26** in tens, units, tenths and hundredths = ______

____

4) **2.51** in units and hundredths = ______________

____

5) **86.514** in units and thousandths = ___________

____

6) **0.228** in thousandths = ______________________

7) **74.98** in hundredths = ______________________

8) **5.48** in units and hundredths = ______________________

____

9) **964.4** in tenths = ______________________

10) **1.6** in tenths = ______________________

Score

e. Decimals in Value Order

It is important to be able to put **Decimals in Value Order**.

Example: Arrange the decimals in size order, smallest first.
0.2 **0.023** **0.51**

Step 1 - Draw a decimal table and place the numbers in it.

Step 2 - Complete the table by filling in the spaces with zeros. This converts all the numbers to thousandths.

U	t	h	th	
0 •	**2**	0	0	→**200 thousandths**
0 •	**0**	**2**	**3**	→**23 thousandths**
0 •	**5**	**1**	0	→**510 thousandths**

Step 3 - Reorder the numbers by size, smallest first.

Answer: **0.023, 0.2, 0.51**

Exercise 3: 5 Write the following decimals in size order, smallest first:

Score

1) **2.9** **0.29** **9.201**

_______ _______ _______

2) **0.005** **0.5** **0.05**

_______ _______ _______

3) **2.8** **2.86** **0.52**

_______ _______ _______

4) **5.63** **3.6** **7.2**

_______ _______ _______

5) **2.71** **6.728** **2.1** 6) **4.86** **1.9** **0.5**

Write the following in size order, largest first:

7) **8.97** **9.4** **9** 8) **4.924** **7.1** **3.486**

9) **1.069** **96.1** **0.96** 10) **0.957** **9.57** **2.79**

The size of decimals can be shown in relation to each other by using the following signs.

< ‘Smaller than’ **>** ‘Bigger than’

Remember: The mouth of the crocodile always swallows the largest amount.

Example:

Smaller than

0.5 < 2.6

Bigger than

2.6 > 0.5

Exercise 3: 6 Place ‘bigger than’ or ‘smaller than’ signs between these numbers:

1) **2.7** **7.7** 2) **0.315** **0.4**

3) **4.01** **0.571** 4) **78.663** **78.636**

5) **0.364** **1.32** 6) **5.690** **5.701**

7) **0.7** **0.85** 8) **0.08** **0.071**

9) **5.48** **4.851** 10) **0.475** **0.97**

Score

f. Number Lines and Decimals

Decimal number sequences can appear confusing unless the smallest counting unit is clearly established.

Example: What number does the arrow point to?

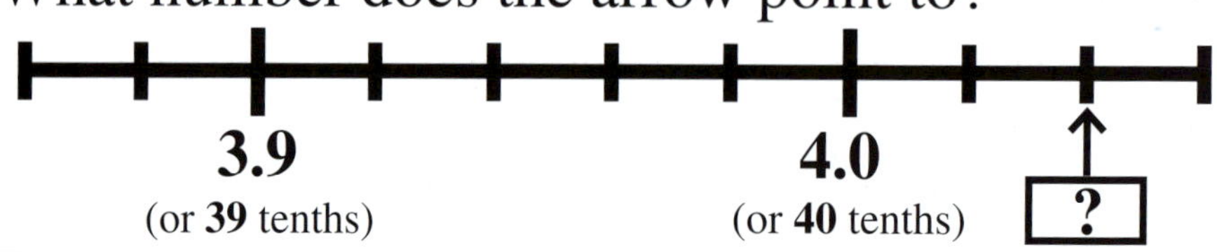

The larger gap between **3.9** and **4.0** is a tenth of a unit (**3.9** has 1 d.p.), so the smaller gaps are in hundredths of a unit.

Step 1 - Add zeros to **3.9 (3.90**) and **4.0 (4.00**) to change them to hundredths of a unit.

Step 2 - Treat **3.90** and **4.00** as whole numbers, i.e. **390** and **400**. Label each missing gap, which is **2** hundredths of a unit.

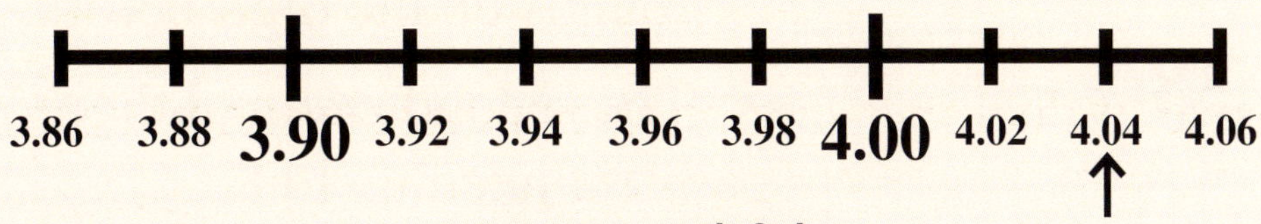

Answer: **4.04**

Exercise 3: 7 Write the numbers indicated:

Change to hundredths.

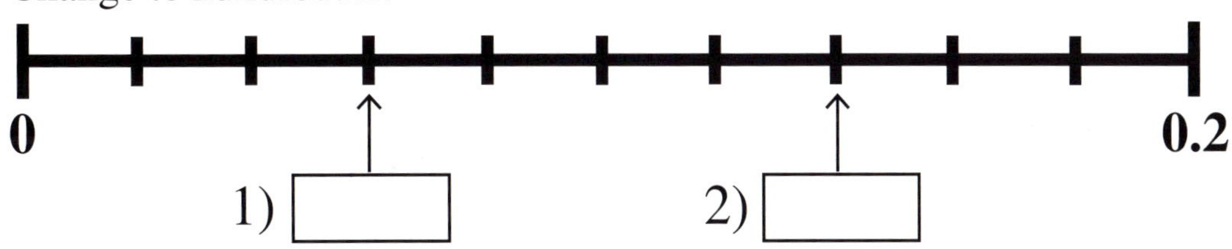

Change to hundredths.

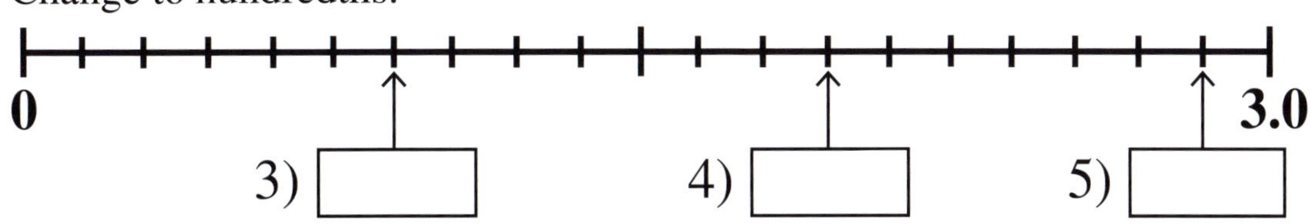

Change to thousandths.

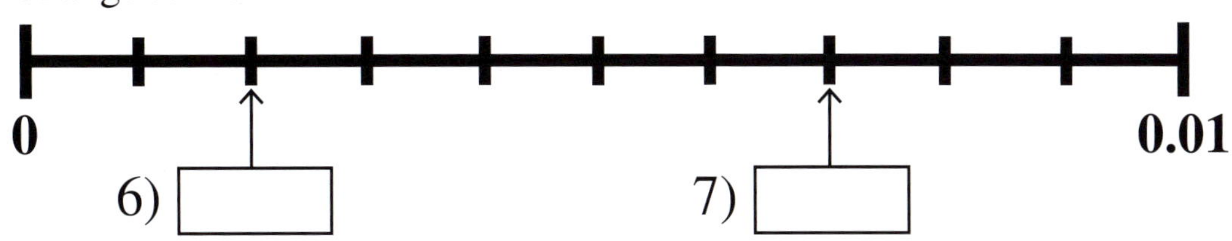

Change to thousandths.

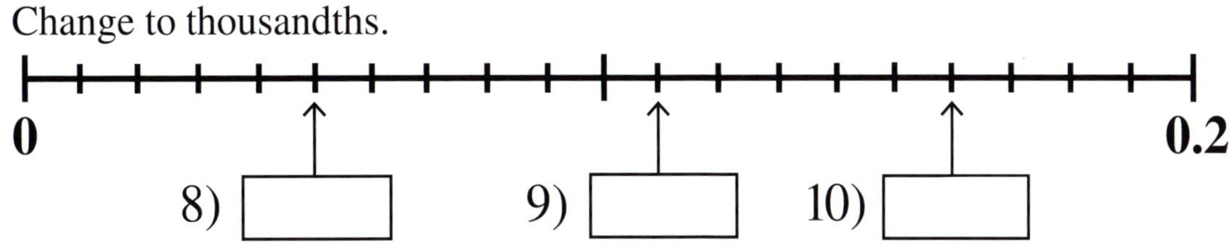

g. Rounding Decimal Values

By **Rounding Decimal Values**, approximate answers can be found. Rounding occurs to a set number of decimal places.

Example 1: Round **5.375** to 2 decimal places.

2 Places | Decider

5.37|**5**

Rounds up to **8**

5.3**8**

- If the third decimal digit (decider) is **5 or above**, it rounds up the digit before.
- The second decimal digit, **7**, is rounded up to **8**.

Answer: **5.38**

Example 2: Round **5.374** to 2 decimal places.

2 Places | Decider

5.37|**4**

No rounding

5.37

- If the third decimal digit (decider) is **4 or below**, it leaves the digit before it unchanged.
- The **7** remains the same.

Answer: **5.37**

Exercise 3: 8 Round the following: **Score**

1) **4.009** to 2 d.p. ______

2) **1.538** to 2 d.p. ______

3) **13.85** to 1 d.p. ______

4) **3.07** to 1 d.p. ______

5) **8.155** to 1 d.p. ______

6) **7.406** to 2 d.p. ______

7) **5.2714** to 3 d.p. ______

8) **5.506** to 2 d.p. ______

9) **4.54** to 1 d.p. ______

10) **4.6981** to 3 d.p. ______

A complication can occur when a **9** has to be rounded.

Example: Round **3.897** to 2 decimal places.

2 Places | Decider

3.89|7

Rounds up to **9**

3.**90**|

- The third digit, **7**, rounds up the **9** to a **10** to give **9** tenths.
- In practice, **pass over the 9** dropping it down to **0**. Then round up the next digit. The **8** becomes a **9**.

Although the **0** in the hundredths column has no value here, it must be included as the question asked for 2 d.p.

Answer: **3.90**

Exercise 3: 9 Round the following:

Score

1) **1.596** to 2 d.p. ______
2) **7.3594** to 3 d.p. ______
3) **87.958** to 1 d.p. ______
4) **5.49** to 1 d.p. ______
5) **2.796** to 2 d.p. ______
6) **5.489** to 2 d.p. ______
7) **2.0049** to 3 d.p. ______
8) **6.4394** to 3 d.p. ______
9) **6.291** to 1 d.p. ______
10) **8.197** to 2 d.p. ______

Round Decimals to tenths, hundredths or thousandths

This is the same as rounding to **1**, **2** or **3** decimal places.

- Round to tenths means round to **1** decimal place.
- Round to hundredths means round to **2** decimal places.
- Round to thousandths means round to **3** decimal places.

Exercise 3: 10 Round to tenths, hundredths or thousandths:

Score

1) **0.92** (tenths) ______
2) **7.283** (hundredths) ______

3) **2.8174** (thousandths) ______ 4) **1.955** (hundredths) ______

5) **6.371** (hundredths) ______ 6) **3.869** (tenths) ______

7) **0.6203** (thousandths) ______ 8) **2.827** (hundredths) ______

9) **0.84** (tenths) ______ 10) **3.9547** (thousandths) ______

Rounding Decimals to Whole Numbers

If the digit after the decimal point is **5 or above** the unit rounds up. If it is **4 or below** it remains the same.

Example: Round **6.62** and **6.47** to whole numbers.

Note: The decider is always the first digit after the decimal point.

Above **5** rounds up the whole number.

6.62 rounds to **7**

Below **5** leaves whole number the same.

6.47 rounds to **6**

Exercise 3: 11 Round to whole numbers:

1) **0.72** ______ 2) **2.571** ______

3) **54.6** ______ 4) **8.788** ______

5) **0.86** ______ 6) **9.22** ______

7) **60.1** ______ 8) **2.617** ______

9) **4.43** ______ 10) **3.02** ______

Score

h. Estimates and Approximations

Estimating is a good way of checking answers.

- Round to 'easy' numbers like **10**, **100** or **1,000**.
- Work out the estimate using these numbers.
- Use the symbol ≈ which means 'nearly equal to'.
- **Right Order of Magnitude** means about the right size. (The magnitude of something is a measurement of its size.)

Example 1: Estimate $\mathbf{51.09 - 1.7^2}$.

$\mathbf{51.09 - 1.7^2} \longrightarrow \mathbf{51 - 2^2} \longrightarrow \mathbf{51 - 4 \approx 47}$

Round the decimals to the nearest unit. Multiply out the square number. Subtract as normal.

If the number is very small it is approximated to zero.

Example 2: Estimate **200.2 + 0.0002**.

$\mathbf{200.2 + 0.0002} \longrightarrow \mathbf{200 + 0 \approx 200}$

Round the decimals to units of 10.

Answer: **200**

(Numbers with a difference of less than 10% would usually be considered to be in the same order of magnitude.)

Exercise 3: 12

Estimate to the nearest whole number:

Score

1) $\mathbf{4.9 + 8.7} \approx$ ______
2) $\mathbf{857.43 - 65.22} \approx$ ______
3) $\mathbf{23.81 \times 8.8} \approx$ ______
4) $\mathbf{308.2 \div 6.5} \approx$ ______
5) $\mathbf{6.7^2 + 4.5} \approx$ ______
6) $\mathbf{91.64 - 7.07} \approx$ ______
7) $\mathbf{4.75 \times 41.4} \approx$ ______
8) $\mathbf{21.41 \div 6.9} \approx$ ______
9) $\mathbf{9.3 \times 8.74} \approx$ ______
10) $\mathbf{8.9^2 \div 3.4} \approx$ ______

3. Addition and Subtraction

The rules of addition and subtraction:

1. Keep the decimal point in line.
2. Fill all the empty spaces with zeros.
3. Add or subtract as normal.

Example 1: Calculate **4.89 + 63.9**.

$$\begin{array}{r} 04.89 \\ 63.90+ \\ \hline 68.79 \\ \hline \end{array}$$

1

Example 2: Calculate **58.8 – 8.72**.

$$\begin{array}{r} 58.{}^{7}\not{8}{}^{1}0 \\ 08.72- \\ \hline 50.08 \\ \hline \end{array}$$

Exercise 3: 13 Set out and calculate. Do not round.

1) **6.9** + **5.7** = _____

2) **26.1** + **0.61** = _____

3) **81.7** – **7.8** = _____

4) **59.1** – **8.65** = _____

5) **60.92** + **13** + **0.093** = _____

6) **7.65** – **0.287** = _____

7) **56.71** – **4.698** = ______

8) **3.99** + **0.692** = ______

9) **749.12** – **493.64** = ______

10) **88.834** – **82.24** = ______

Score

4. Multiplication

a. Decimal Multiplication

For **Decimal Multiplication** leave out the decimal point whilst doing the sum and replace it after completion.

Example: Calculate **52.8** × **0.52**.

Step 1 - Leave out the decimal points when multiplying.
52.8 becomes **528**
0.52 becomes **52** (the zero on **052** is irrelevant).

Step 2 - The calculation is **528** × **52**.

Use standard column multiplication to solve.

This will give the answer **27,456**.

		5	**2**	**8**	
			5	**2**	×
	1	**0**	$\mathbf{5}_1$	**6**	
2	$\mathbf{6}_1$	$\mathbf{4}_4$	**0**	**0**	
2	**7**	**4**	**5**	**6**	

Step 3 - Count the decimal places in both the original numbers.

$$5\,2\,.\,8 \times 0\,.\,5\,2$$

(1 decimal place in 52.8; 2 decimal places in 0.52)

Step 4 - Add the number of decimal places together.

1 + **2** = **3** decimal places

Step 5 - Count three places from the right in the answer and insert the decimal point.

Count in the point, **3** places from the right.

27 . 4 5 6

Answer: **27.456**

Exercise 3: 14

Round (where necessary) to two decimal places:

1) **8.7** × **4** = _____

2) **3.8** × **0.8** = _____

3) **8.9** × **7** = _____

4) **5.5** × **9** = _____

5) **0.8** × **0.5** = _____

6) **9.4** × **6.6** = _____

7) **0.37** × **1.4** = _____

8) **29.55** × **1.9** = _____

9) **1.6** × **6.2** = _____

10) **0.4** × **0.02** = _____

b. Multiplying Decimals by Tens

Multiplying by ten moves the decimal point **one place to the right**. Each multiplication by ten takes the decimal point one place further to the right.

Example: Calculate **0.4** × **10** and **0.4** × **100**.

These sums can be written:

Multiply by **10** (move d.p. one place).

1 place right →

$$0.40 \times 10 = 04.0 = 4$$

Multiply by **100** (move d.p. two places).

2 places right →

$$0.40 \times 100 = 040.0 = 40$$

To assist in counting the point it helps to add zeros.

Add zeros ↙

0.400 becomes **040.0** Decimal point moves 2 places to the right.

Answer: **4** and **40**

Exercise 3: 15 Calculate the following:

Score

1) **6.9** × **10** = _____ 2) **1.72** × **10** = _____

3) **64.62** × **100** = _____ 4) **3.8** × **100** = _____

5) **59** × **10** = _____ 6) **10.64** × **10** = _____

7) **89.549** × **100** = _____ 8) **2.6** × **1,000** = _____

9) **0.2** × **100** = _____ 10) **91.37** × **1,000** = _____

5. Division

a. Decimal Division

(i) Dividing by a Whole Number

Dividing into a decimal by a whole number follows the same rules as standard division.

It is important to know that **Remainders** and **Decimals** are not the same:

A remainder is a whole number that is left over. ⟶ **18 ÷ 4**

For example, **18 ÷ 4 = 4 groups of 4 units and 2 units left over.**

$$4\overline{)1\,8}\quad = 4 \text{ rem. } 2$$

A decimal is created by carrying the remainder into the tenths column. It is divided to give a decimal answer. ⟶ **18 ÷ 4**

For example, **18 ÷ 4 = 4 groups of 4 units and 5 tenths.**

$$4\overline{)1\,8\,.\,{}^{2}0}\quad = 4.5$$

Example: Calculate **8.1 ÷ 12**. (Round to 2 d.p.)

Step 1 - Set out the calculation as a standard division.

Step 2 - Divide, keeping the decimal point in line in the answer.

Insert extra zeros to allow the division to continue.

Step 3 - Round the answer to 2 decimal places.

0.675 rounds up to **0.68**.

$$
\begin{array}{r}
0.675 \\
12\overline{\smash{)}8.100} \\
\underline{7\,2} \\
90 \\
\underline{84} \\
60 \\
\underline{60} \\
00
\end{array}
$$

Answer: **0.68**

Follow the same technique for short and long division.

Exercise 3: 16

Calculate the following:

(Questions 1-2 divide exactly to 1 or 2 decimal places.)

1) **73.8 ÷ 2**

$$2\overline{\smash{)}73.8}$$

= ________

2) **40.8 ÷ 12**

$$12\overline{\smash{)}40.8}$$

= ________

(Round each answer to 1 decimal place in questions 3-4.)

3) **51.2 ÷ 3**

= ________

4) **42.71 ÷ 21**

= ________

(Round each answer to 2 decimal places in questions 5-8.)

5) **$87.1 \div 6$** = ________

6) **$7.66 \div 22$** = ________

7) **$7.62 \div 23$** = ________

8) **$3.57 \div 8$** = ________

(Round each answer to 3 decimal places in questions 9-10.)

9) **$0.211 \div 18$** = ________

10) **$5.035 \div 17$** = ________

Score

(ii) Dividing by a Decimal

In **Decimal Division**, the divisor (dividing number) must be a whole number. If the divisor is a decimal:

1. Move the decimal point in the divisor to the right, making it a whole number.
2. Compensate by moving the decimal point in the

dividend (number being divided into) to the right by the same number of places.

3. Do the calculation as normal. Follow the same technique for short and long division.

Example: Calculate **8.25 ÷ 0.6**.

Step 1 - Move the decimal point one place to the right on the divisor and dividend.

Move 1 place → **8.25** ÷ Move 1 place → **0.6**

Step 2 - This is now **17.3** divided by **7** units.

82.5 ÷ 6

Step 3 - Add some zeros to enable the division to continue. Round to 2 decimal places.

$$6\overline{)8^{2}2.{}^{4}5{}^{3}0} = 13.75$$

Answer: **13.75**

Exercise 3: 17a Calculate the following:

(Questions 1-4 divide exactly to two decimal places.)

1) **7.56 ÷ 1.5**

$$15\overline{)75.60}$$

= ________

2) **0.288 ÷ 2.4**

$$24\overline{)2.88}$$

= ________

3) **0.344 ÷ 0.4**

= ________

4) **1.47 ÷ 0.04**

= ________

(ii) Recurring Decimals

Some numbers that will not divide exactly will produce a **Recurring Decimal**. This is a number that has a repeated pattern that will go on the same way forever.

Example 1: Calculate **17.2 ÷ 6.**

Divide the decimal the same way as before.

$$\begin{array}{r} 2.8666 \\ 6\,\overline{)\,17.{}^{5}2{}^{4}0{}^{4}0{}^{4}0} \end{array}$$

The answer can be shown with a **recurring dot**.

$$2.8\dot{6}$$

It can also be rounded to 2 d.p. **2.87**

Exercise 3: 17b Calculate the following:

(Use a recurring dot to show recurring decimals in questions 5-6.)

5) **77.2 ÷ 0.03**

= ________

6) **1.87 ÷ 0.06**

= ________

(Round each answer to 2 decimal places in questions 7-8.)

7) **2.01 ÷ 0.7**

= ________

8) **76.3 ÷ 0.23**

= ________

(Round each answer to 3 decimal places in questions 9-10.)

9) **65.5 ÷ 1.7**

= ________

10) **1.99 ÷ 0.14**

= ________

Score

(iii) Hidden Decimals

If there are no decimals in a question but they appear in the answer, they are called **Hidden Decimals**.

Example: Calculate **63 ÷ 4**.

Step 1 - No decimal points are shown in the question. Complete as standard short division.

$$\begin{array}{r} 15.75 \\ 4\overline{)63.{}^{3}0{}^{2}0} \end{array}$$

Step 2 - Insert a decimal point and extra zero to continue the division. The answer has two decimal places.

Answer: **15.75**

Exercise 3: 18 Calculate the following:

Score

Answer to 2 decimal places where necessary.

1) **17 ÷ 8** = ______

$8\overline{)17.0}$

2) **23 ÷ 6** = ______

$6\overline{)23.00}$

3) **34 ÷ 3** = ______

4) **96 ÷ 5** = ______

5) **85 ÷ 3** = ______

6) **14 ÷ 9** = ______

7) **54 ÷ 7** = ______

8) **92 ÷ 9** = ______

9) **43 ÷ 2** = ______

10) **17 ÷ 6** = ______

b. Dividing Decimals by Tens

Dividing by Ten moves the decimal point **one place to the left**. Each division by ten takes the decimal point one place further to the left.

Example: Calculate **0.6 ÷ 10** and **0.6 ÷ 100**.

These sums can be written:

Divide by **10**
(move d.p. one place).

1 place left ←

$$\mathbf{0.6 \div 10 = 0.06}$$

Divide by **100**
(move d.p. two places).

2 places left ←

$$\mathbf{0.6 \div 100 = 0.006}$$

To assist in counting the point it helps to add zeros.

Add zeros ↘ **000.6** becomes **0.006** Decimal point moves 2 places to the left.

Answer: **0.06** and **0.006**

Exercise 3: 19 Calculate the following: **Score**

1) **13.8 ÷ 10** = ______ 2) **39.4 ÷ 100** = ______

3) **25 ÷ 10** = ______ 4) **97 ÷ 100** = ______

5) **2.39 ÷ 100** = ______ 6) **66.4 ÷ 10** = ______

7) **53.2 ÷ 100** = ______ 8) **24.5 ÷ 1,000** = ______

9) **15.9 ÷ 100** = ______ 10) **0.5 ÷ 100** = ______

6. Decimal Operations
a. Decimal Tables

Decimal Tables work in the same way as addition, subtraction, multiplication and division tables, except decimal values are used (see earlier in Maths Workbook 1).

Exercise 3: 20 Find the missing amounts: Score

1-2)
A = ____
B = ____

+	8.9	9.6
A	10.1	10.8
3.3	12.2	**B**

3-4)
A = ____
B = ____

−	9.9	7.9
A	7.5	5.5
3.8	6.1	**B**

5-7)
A = ____
B = ____
C = ____

×	0.3	0.4	**A**
6	**B**	2.4	4.8
8	2.4	3.2	6.4
9	2.7	**C**	7.2

8-10)
A = ____
B = ____
C = ____

÷	**A**	15	24
2	6.5	**B**	12
3	$4.\dot{3}$	5	8
C	7.6	3	4.8

b. Order of Operations
(i) With Brackets

If a question contains **Brackets**, do the sum in the brackets first.

Example: Calculate **8.16 ÷ (7.23 − 3.83)**.

Brackets first **7.23 − 3.83 = 3.4** then **8.16 ÷ 3.4 = 2.4**

Answer: **2.4**

Exercise 3: 21a Calculate the following to 2 d.p.:

1) $\mathbf{6.58} \div (\mathbf{2.1} \times \mathbf{0.3})$

= _________

2) $(\mathbf{5.3} + \mathbf{0.37}) \times \mathbf{9.2}$

= _________

3) $(\mathbf{0.54} \times \mathbf{0.4}) + \mathbf{6.42}$

= _________

4) $\mathbf{3.1} \div (\mathbf{0.11} - \mathbf{0.008})$

= _________

5) $\mathbf{0.14} \times (\mathbf{7.6} - \mathbf{1.14})$ = _________

(ii) Without Brackets

The Order of Operations can be remembered by using the acronym **BIDMAS** (sometimes seen as **BODMAS**).

Brackets, **I**ndices, **D**ivision, **M**ultiplication, **A**ddition and **S**ubtraction

or **O**f (to the power 'of')

If a sum has no brackets or indices but has two or more signs, do ÷ or × first (in the order of the question), then + or – (in the order of the question).

Example: Calculate **8.4** – **6** × **0.7**.

Multiply first **6** × **0.7** = **4.2** then **8.4** – **4.2** = **4.2**

Answer: **4.2**

Exercise 3: 21b Calculate the following to 2 d.p.:

6) $\mathbf{7.7} + \mathbf{5} - \mathbf{0.4}$

= _________

7) $\mathbf{2} + \mathbf{0.24} \times \mathbf{2.3}$

= _________

8) $\mathbf{7.2} - \mathbf{0.5} + \mathbf{2}$

= _________

9) $\mathbf{8} \div \mathbf{0.25} - \mathbf{0.93}$

= _________

10) $\mathbf{0.18} \times \mathbf{6.5} \div \mathbf{5}$ = _________

Score

7. Decimal Problems

Remember the following definitions:

Add → **Sum** Subtract → **Difference**

Multiply → **Product** Divide → **Quotient**

Exercise 3: 22 Do the following calculations:

Score

1) Find the sum of **84.38** and **1.62**. ________

2) Find the difference between **37.2** and **5.3**. ________

3) Find the product of **62** and **1.3**. ________

4) Find the quotient of **29.7** by **3.3**. ________

This table shows the marks scored by **three** children in their end of year tests.

Subject	Sheila	Moses	Vicky
History	**23.6**	**30**	**20.6**
Geography	**28.4**	**36.3**	**25.5**
Economics	**50.8**	**40.4**	**78.8**

5) Who scored the lowest score in any subject? ________

6) What was the highest score achieved in any subject? ________

7) Which child scored the most overall? ________

8) Who scored the least overall? ________

9) Find the sum of **59.1** and **4.9** then divide it by the difference between **1.5** and **5.3**. Give your answer to 2 d.p. ________

10) Find the difference between **2.8** and **3.5** then multiply it by **9.2**. ________

Answers

Chapter One
Basic Number

Exercise 1: 1
1) 68 2) 818 3) 500,000
4) 568 5) 1,081 6) 46,000
7) 7,884 8) 204,840
9) 11,000 10) 5,820,529

Exercise 1: 2
1) Thirty-one 2) Sixty-nine
3) Two hundred and ninety-six
4) Five hundred and ninety
5) Five hundred and twenty-nine
6) Four thousand, seven hundred and eighty-six
7) Thirty-five thousand, seven hundred and one
8) Fifty-seven thousand, four hundred and fifty
9) Nine hundred and sixty-four thousand, four hundred and two
10) Two million, ninety-three thousand, four hundred and eighty two

Exercise 1: 3
1) 9,886; 7,450; 3,211; 1,364; 463; 194
2) One ten; Nine hundreds
3) 80,000; 7; 8,000
4) 265,922 5) 83,323
6) 965; 956; 695; 659; 596; 569
7) 327,619 8) 29,033
9) 33; 99; 786; 1,526; 7,870; 8,701
10) 23,669

Exercise 1: 4a
1) 7,327 2) 9,194
3) 10,891 4) 12,809

Exercise 1: 4b
(Missing numbers only)
5) 9; 8; 3 6) 6; 1; 7
7) 1; 9; 9 8) 1; 5; 4
9) 6; 8; 2 10) 9; 2; 1

Exercise 1: 5a
1) 6,408 2) 9,211
3) 6,387 4) 5,487

Exercise 1: 5b
5) 35 6) 207
7) 3,616 8) 2,514
9) 3,471 10) 3,837

Exercise 1: 6
1) 215 2) 589 3) 658
4) 6,268 5) 7,733 6) 3,532
7) 4,185 8) 5,445
9) 11,388 10) 32,538

Exercise 1: 7
(Missing numbers only)
1) 0; 2; 4 2) 4; 8; 7
3) 0; 7; 1 4) 6; 6; 9
5) 7; 9; 3; 3 6) 8; 3; 7; 3
7) 5; 9; 7; 1 8) 8; 2; 1; 9
9) 2; 0; 8; 2 10) 4; 5; 1; 6

Exercise 1: 8a
1) 64,719 2) 38,255
3) 24,765 4) 45,078
5) 11,905 6) 28,844

Exercise 1: 8b
(Missing numbers only)
7) 5; 1 8) 6; 4
9) 5; 9 10) 8; 8

Exercise 1: 9
1) 40 2) 900
3) 8,000 4) 2,700
5) 700 6) 80,000
7) 13,000 8) 33,000
9) 9,200 10) 30,000

Exercise 1: 10
1) 2,108 2) 3,300
3) 1,827 4) 3,969
5) 42,845 6) 44,252
7) 38,930 8) 26,376
9) 97,380 10) 684,410

Exercise 1: 11
1) 1,656 2) 720
3) 1,896 4) 1,664
5) 11,232 6) 70,272
7) 27,132 8) 96,222
9) 202,932 10) 439,064

Exercise 1: 12a
1) 69 2) 156
3) 71 4) 1,054 r. 4
5) 386 r. 1 6) 5,340 r. 5

Exercise 1: 12b
(Missing numbers only)
7) 1 8) 1 9) 8 10) 7

Exercise 1: 13
1) 2 2) 7 3) 90
4) 44 5) 5 6) 390
7) 80 8) 65 9) 70
10) 42

Exercise 1: 14
1) 231 2) 524
3) 84 4) 236
5) 399 r. 12 6) 62 r. 22
7) 704 r. 1 8) 1,185 r.16
9) 1,727 r. 6 10) 2,472 r.15

Exercise 1: 15
1) 48 2) 129 3) 64
4) 95 5) 21 6) 125
7) 96 8) 2 9) 6
10) 1,422

Exercise 1: 16
1-2) 125; 93
3-5) 72; 159; 87
6-7) 527; 31
8-10) 3,864; 46; 84

Answers

Exercise 1: 17a
1) 85 2) 6 3) 80
4) 343 5) 3

Exercise 1: 17b
6) 21 7) 19 8) 21
9) 1 10) 85

Exercise 1: 18a
1) 56 2) 123 3) 8
4) 193 5) 204

Exercise 1: 18b
6) 137 7) 99 8) 132
9) 24 10) 6

Exercise 1: 19
1) 7; 8; 6; 1 2) 171
3) 4,320,000 4) 699,548
5) 12 6) 187
7) 3,791 8) 18,175
9) 170 10) 99

Chapter Two
Number Relationships

Exercise 2: 1
1) A = 4 2) A = 19
3-4) A = 8 ; B = 20
5-6) A = 24 ; B = 22
7-8) A = 20 ; B = 19
9-10) A = 70 ; B = 10

Exercise 2: 2
1-2) A = 12; B = 14
3-4) A = 4; B = 6
5-7) A = 17; B = 19; C = 22
8-10) A = 4; B = 15; C = 33

Exercise 2: 3
1-2) A = 20; B = 3
3-4) A = 12; B = 9
5-7) A = 19; B = 23; C = 13
8-10) A = 5; B = 2; C = 18

Exercise 2: 4
1-2) A = 42; B = 8
3-4) A = 24; B = 6
5-7) A = 11; B = 18
C = 108
8-10) A = 4; B = 20
C = 7

Exercise 2: 5
1-2) A = 30; B = 6
3-4) A = 16; B = 8
5-7) A = 24; B = 9; C = 4
8-10) A = 36; B = 8; C = 12

Exercise 2: 6
1) 20 2) 960
3) 200 4) 400
5) 8,000 6) 7,000
7) 80 8) 240
9) 620 10) 9

Exercise 2: 7
1) even 2) odd
3) even 4) odd
5) even 6) odd
7) even 8) even
9) 32; 898; 440; 976; 38
10) does

Exercise 2: 8
1) 25 2) 36
3) 64 4) 100
5) 144 6) 169
7) 196 8) 225
9) 400 10) 576

Exercise 2: 9
1) 10 2) 6
3) 8 4) 2
5) 3 6) 11
7) 12 8) 5
9) 7 10) 9

Exercise 2: 10
1) 125 2) 1,331
3) 343 4) 216
5) 1,000 6) 8
7) 64 8) 27
9) 512 10) 1,728

Exercise 2: 11
1) prime 2) not prime
3) prime 4) not prime
5) not prime 6) prime
7) not prime 8) not prime
9) not prime 10) prime

Exercise 2: 12
1) no 2) no 3) yes
4) no 5) yes 6) no
7) 18 8) 10 9) 35 10) 21

Exercise 2: 13
1) 21 2) 55 3) 36
4) 28 5) 15 6) 45
7) 21 and 15 8) 36 and 6
9) 6 and 1 10) 15 and 3

Exercise 2: 14a
1) 40, 8 2) 36, 31
3) 27, 44 4) 16, 64
5) 20, 22 6) 4, 2

Exercise 2: 14b
7) 7, 9 8) 5, 6
9) 13, 16 10) 15, 21

Exercise 2: 15
1) 60 2) 210 3) 50
4) 175 5) 30 6) 90
7) 170 8) 16
9) 64 10) 128

Exercise 2: 16a
1) 8 2) 5
3) -4°C 4) -1°C
5) 11°C

Exercise 2: 16b
6) a) < b) < c) >
7) -9, -4, -1, 2, 6, 7, 9

Exercise 2: 16c
8) 16 9) 2 10) -15

Answers

Exercise 2: 17

1) 1, 2, 4, 5, 10, 20
2) 1, 2, 3, 4, 6, 12
3) 1, 2, 11, 22
4) 1, 2, 4, 7, 14, 28
5) 1, 5, 11, 55
6) 1, 2, 3, 4, 6, 8, 12, 16, 24, 48
7) 1, 2, 3, 4, 6, 7, 12, 14, 21, 28, 42, 84
8) 1, 5, 17, 85
9) 1, 5, 19, 95
10) 1, 3, 17, 51

Exercise 2: 18a

1) 3 2) 1, 3, 7, 21
3) 7 4) 3, 5, 15

Exercise 2: 18b

5) 7 6) 39
7) 5 8) 11
9) 12 10) 14

Exercise 2: 19

1)
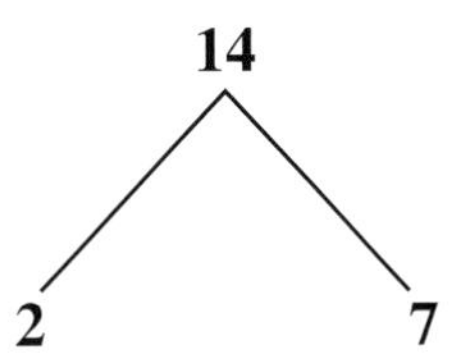

2)
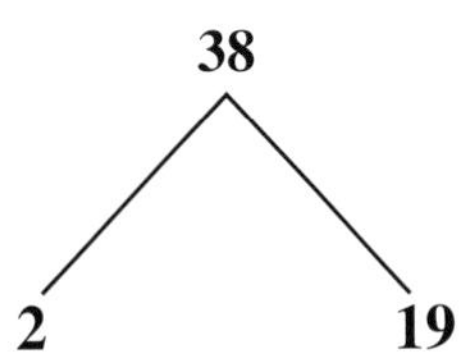

3)
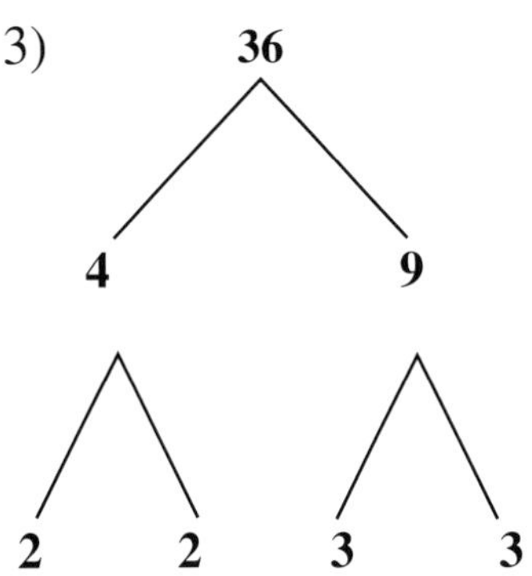

4)
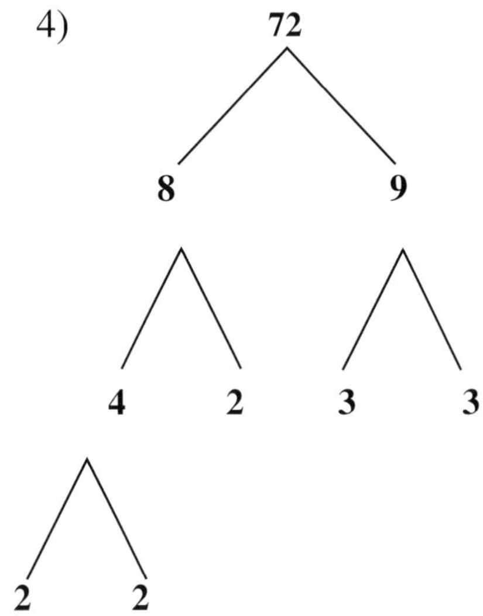

5)
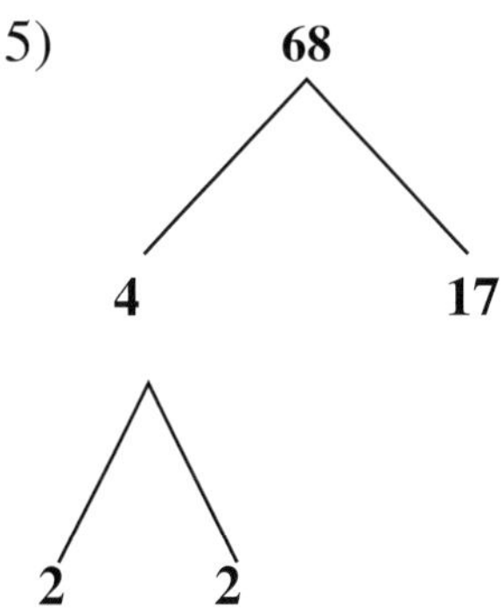

6)
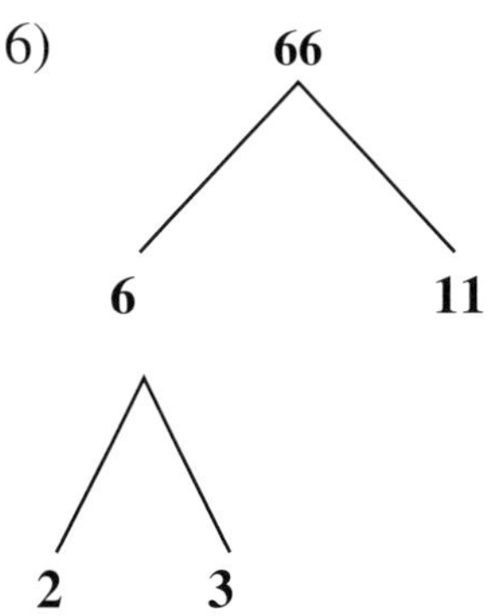

7) 3 8) 5^2
9) 11 10) 7

Exercise 2: 20

1) 18, 27, 36, 45, 54
2) 26, 39, 52, 65, 78
3) 28, 42, 56, 70, 84
4) 6, 9, 12, 15, 18
5) 24, 36, 48, 60, 72
6) 14, 21, 28, 35, 42
7) 30, 45, 60, 75, 90
8) 4, 6, 8, 10, 12
9) 16, 24, 32, 40, 48
10) 38, 57, 76, 95, 114

Exercise 2: 21a

1) 12, 24 2) 30, 60
3) 22, 44 4) 24, 48

Exercise 2: 21b

5) 28 6) 63
7) 12 8) 24
9) 24 10) 8

Exercise 2: 22

1) 1,500
2) 6
3) 186
4) 110
5) 217
6) 47
7) 18
8) 138
9) 14
10) 96

Exercise 2: 23

1) 18
2) 479
3) 785
4) 357
5) 1,007
6) 1,971
7) 1,455
8) 2,894
9) 3,825
10) 975

Exercise 2: 24

1) LVI 2) XIII
3) CDVI 4) XLI
5) DCCXXXV
6) DCCCLXXI
7) MCCXIV

Answers

8) MCCCVIII
9) MMMDCCLXX
10) MDXLII

Exercise 2: 25

1) a) A = 15; B = 16
   b) A = 43; B = 41
2) a) 225 b) 64
   c) 729 d) 10
3) a) 1, 3, 6, 10, 15
   b) 6, 10, 15 c) 36 d) 21
4) a) 125, 216 b) 48, 80
5) a) 17 b) -2 c) 4
6) a) 1, 2, 4, 7, 14, 28 b) 12
   c) $2^2 \times 3^2$ d) 2
7) a) 72 b) 60 c) 66
8) 204 seats
9) 128 marbles
10) 20 bottles

Chapter Three
Decimals

Exercise 3: 1

1) 8.0 2) 34.0
3) 69.0 4) 504.0
5) 9,590.0 6) 5
7) 84 8) 37
9) 765 10) 7,958

Exercise 3: 2

	TH	H	T	U •	t	h	th
1)			4	0 •	2	8	
2)				1 •	2	6	7
3)		5	2	5 •	7		
4)			2	0 •	6	4	0
5)	6	2	4	3 •	9	0	6
6)				7 •	3		
7)				6 •	4	2	
8)				0 •	2	5	6
9)		5	4	1 •	7	1	
10)	4	5	3	9 •	5	3	0

Exercise 3: 3

1) 5 tenths
2) 8 hundredths
3) 6 hundredths
4) 3 units 5) 9 tens
6) 1 tenth
7) $0.75\underline{8}$ 8) $\underline{5}.06$
9) $7.1\underline{8}$ 10) $7.\underline{5}63$

Exercise 3: 4

1) 8,981 thousandths
2) 575 hundredths
3) 7 tens, 8 units, 2 tenths and 6 hundredths
4) 2 units and 51 hundredths
5) 86 units and 514 thousandths
6) 228 thousandths
7) 7,498 hundredths
8) 5 units and 48 hundredths
9) 9,644 tenths
10) 16 tenths

Exercise 3: 5

1) 0.29; 2.9; 9.201
2) 0.005; 0.05; 0.5
3) 0.52; 2.8; 2.86
4) 3.6; 5.63; 7.2
5) 2.1; 2.71; 6.728
6) 0.5; 1.9; 4.86
7) 9.4; 9; 8.97
8) 7.1; 4.924; 3.486
9) 96.1; 1.069, 0.96
10) 9.57; 2.79; 0.957

Exercise 3: 6

1) 2.7 < 7.7
2) 0.315 < 0.4
3) 4.01 > 0.571
4) 78.663 > 78.636
5) 0.364 < 1.32
6) 5.690 < 5.701
7) 0.7 < 0.85
8) 0.08 > 0.071
9) 5.48 > 4.851
10) 0.475 < 0.97

Exercise 3: 7

1) 0.06 2) 0.14
3) 0.9 4) 1.95
5) 2.85 6) 0.002
7) 0.007 8) 0.05
9) 0.11 10) 0.16

Exercise 3: 8

1) 4.01 2) 1.54
3) 13.9 4) 3.1
5) 8.2 6) 7.41
7) 5.271 8) 5.51
9) 4.5 10) 4.698

Exercise 3: 9

1) 1.60 2) 7.359
3) 88.0 4) 5.5
5) 2.80 6) 5.49
7) 2.005 8) 6.439
9) 6.3 10) 8.20

Exercise 3: 10

1) 0.9 2) 7.28
3) 2.817 4) 1.96
5) 6.37 6) 3.9
7) 0.620 8) 2.83
9) 0.8 10) 3.955

Exercise 3: 11

1) 1 2) 3
3) 55 4) 9
5) 1 6) 9
7) 60 8) 3
9) 4 10) 3

Exercise 3: 12

1) 14 2) 792
3) 216 4) 44
5) 54 6) 85
7) 205 8) 3
9) 81 10) 27

Answers

Exercise 3: 13
1) 12.6 2) 26.71
3) 73.9 4) 50.45
5) 74.013 6) 7.363
7) 52.012 8) 4.682
9) 255.48 10) 6.594

Exercise 3: 14
1) 34.8 2) 3.04
3) 62.3 4) 49.5
5) 0.4 6) 62.04
7) 0.52 8) 56.15
9) 9.92 10) 0.01

Exercise 3: 15
1) 69 2) 17.2
3) 6,462 4) 380
5) 590 6) 106.4
7) 8,954.9 8) 2,600
9) 20 10) 91,370

Exercise 3: 16
1) 36.9 2) 3.4
3) 17.1 4) 2.0
5) 14.52 6) 0.35
7) 0.33 8) 0.45
9) 0.012 10) 0.296

Exercise 3: 17a
1) 5.04 2) 0.12
3) 0.86 4) 36.75

Exercise 3: 17b
5) 2,573.3 6) 31.16
7) 2.87 8) 331.74
9) 38.529 10) 14.214

Exercise 3: 18
1) 2.13 2) 3.83
3) 11.33 4) 19.2
5) 28.33 6) 1.56
7) 7.71 8) 10.22
9) 21.5 10) 2.83

Exercise 3: 19
1) 1.38 2) 0.394
3) 2.5 4) 0.97
5) 0.0239 6) 6.64
7) 0.532 8) 0.0245
9) 0.159 10) 0.005

Exercise 3: 20
1) A = 1.2 2) B = 12.9
3) A = 2.4 4) B = 4.1
5) A = 0.8 6) B = 1.8
7) C = 3.6 8) A = 13
9) B = 7.5 10) C = 5

Exercise 3: 21a
1) 10.44 2) 52.16
3) 6.64 4) 30.39
5) 0.90

Exercise 3: 21b
6) 12.3 7) 2.55
8) 8.7 9) 31.07
10) 0.23

Exercise 3: 22
1) 86 2) 31.9
3) 80.6 4) 9
5) Vicky scored lowest
6) 78.8 in Economics
7) Vicky scored most
8) Sheila scored least
9) 16.84 10) 6.44

PROGRESS CHARTS

Shade in your score for each exercise on the graph. Add up for your total score. If there are a) b) c) etc. parts to a question, all parts must be correct to gain a mark.

1. BASIC NUMBER

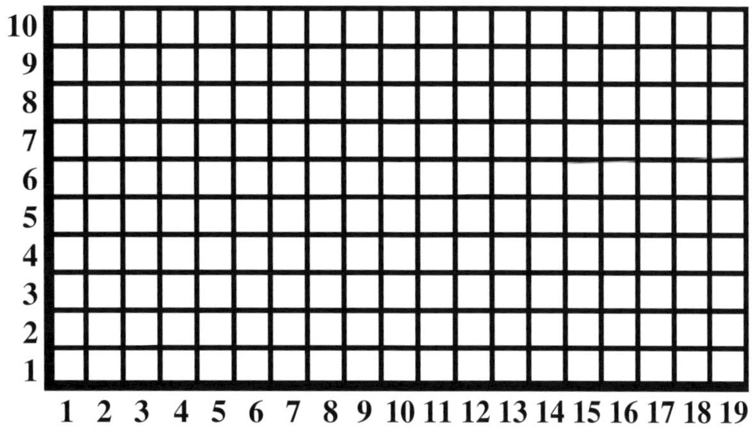

Total Score

Percentage %

2. NUMBER RELATIONSHIPS

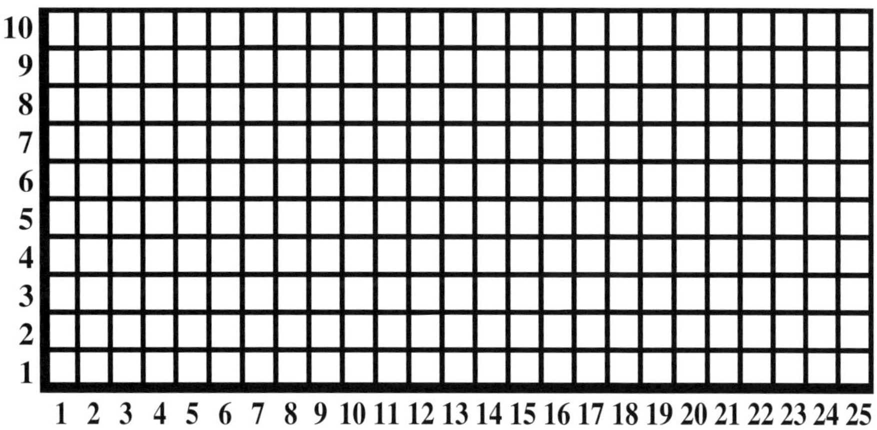

Total Score

Percentage %

3. DECIMALS

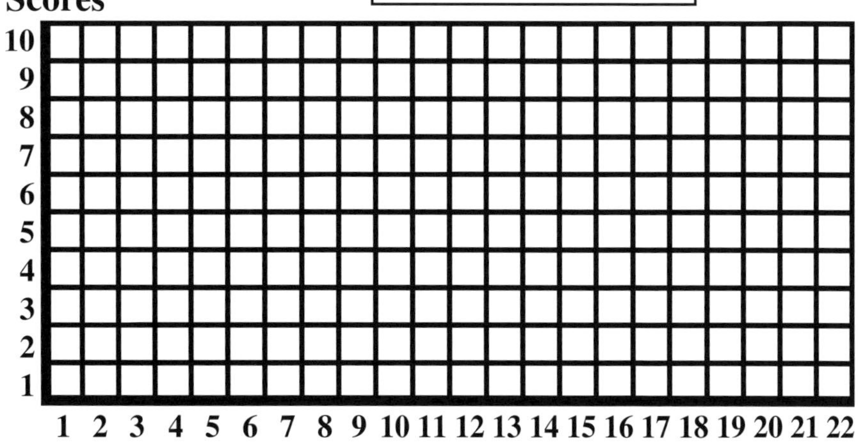

Total Score

Percentage %

For the average add up % and divide by 3

Overall Percentage %

CERTIFICATE OF

ACHIEVEMENT

This certifies

____

has successfully completed

KS2 Maths

Year 5/6

WORKBOOK **1**

Overall percentage score achieved ______ %

Comment ______________________________

____

Signed ______________________________

(teacher/parent/guardian)

Date ______________________________

SUCCESSFUL ae COMPLETION